· WARD LOCK MASTER GARDENER ·

# The Gardening Y

JANE COURTIER

**WARD LOCK**

First published in Great Britain in 1993
by Ward Lock Limited, Villiers House, 41/47 Strand,
London WC2N 5JE, England

A Cassell Imprint

British Library Cataloguing in Publication Data is
available upon application to The British Library

ISBN 0 7063 7137 2

Text filmset by Litho Link Ltd, Welshpool, Powys
Printed and bound in Singapore by Craft Print Pte Ltd

*Previous page:* **A mixture of
spring bulbs, forget-me-nots
and pansies creates a splash
of colour early in the year.**

# Contents

# Preface

Even the keenest and most knowledgeable gardener sometimes needs a reminder of the jobs to be done throughout the year – it's so easy to forget all the things you intend to try. There's no point remembering in early spring that you wanted to experiment with autumn-sown broad beans this year, or that you were going to try your own spring bedding from seed.

I hope that this book will prove to be a useful memory jogger for the major tasks in the garden, though of course it cannot hope to cover every facet of such a wonderfully wide and varied hobby as gardening. If I have left out something you specially wanted to know about, I apologise – but perhaps you might find something interesting that you *hadn't* considered, in its place!

I hope that gardeners and plant lovers might also use this book to remind themselves of the delights of other seasons. Flicking through the pages in winter, you can look forward to the first signs of spring, and the warm and busy days of summer. In autumn, you may be cheered by descriptions of the many plants that are decorative in the depths of winter, and perhaps inspired

◀ **Keeping evergreen foliage in a container near the house provides interest in the garden even in the depths of winter.**

to plant some for your own dose of winter sunshine.

I have deliberately avoided putting specific months to the seasons in this book. If you are gardening in a warm, southerly region, you will find spring comes much earlier than in cooler, northerly areas. And if you happen to be reading this in the southern hemisphere, of course, the months would make no sense to you at all. Even within a few miles, there can be quite a difference in the time of the last frost between one garden and another, and then, of course, every year is different, too. There's no need to argue about the exact week that mid-spring turns into late spring, or that summer turns into autumn; gardening is not a precision science. In any case, anyone who is in tune with growing things, who uses their five senses each time they step outside, will not need telling when the first crisp, clear day of autumn arrives, or when winter finally gives up its grip and surrenders to spring.

Every gardener makes mistakes sometimes, and has disappointments as well as wonderful rewards. But one of the best things about gardening is the fact the seasons roll gently but relentlessly on, each season bringing with it a whole new set of challenges, rewards and opportunities. Enjoy your gardening – all through the year!

J.C.

## PUBLISHER'S NOTES

Readers are requested to note that, in order to make the text intelligible in both hemispheres, timings are generally described in terms of seasons not months. In some instances, e.g. in some tables, it is not practicable to use seasons and the months cited are for the northern hemisphere. However, by using the following table the reader can easily translate timings of seasons or months from one hemisphere to another.

| Northern Hemisphere | | | | Southern Hemisphere |
|---|---|---|---|---|
| Mid-winter | = | January | = | Mid-summer |
| Late winter | = | February | = | Late summer |
| Early spring | = | March | = | Early autumn |
| Mid-spring | = | April | = | Mid-autumn |
| Late spring | = | May | = | Late autumn |
| Early summer | = | June | = | Early winter |
| Mid-summer | = | July | = | Mid-winter |
| Late summer | = | August | = | Late winter |
| Early autumn | = | September | = | Early spring |
| Mid-autumn | = | October | = | Mid-spring |
| Late autumn | = | November | = | Late spring |
| Early winter | = | December | = | Early summer |

## ACKNOWLEDGEMENTS

The publishers would like to thank the following for supplying photographs for this book: *Amateur Gardening* magazine: pp. 12, 20, 21, 41, 56, 57, 61, 69, 88; Pat Brindley: p. 49; Photos Horticultural Picture Library: pp. 4, 8, 16, 17, 25, 28, 32, 37, 40, 52, 64, 65, 68, 72 (left), 77, 81, 89; Kenneth Scowen: pp. 24, 29; Harry Smith: pp. 1, 44, 48, 72 (right), 73, 80, 84, 85, 92, 93.

The line illustrations were drawn by Nils Solberg; the chapter opening decorations by David Woodroffe.

# · 1 ·
# Spring

Spring is a wonderful time for a gardener – a time of new life, new beginnings, and new chances. After a long season of inactivity, when nearly everything in the garden seems to be dormant, gardeners note each small sign of spring eagerly.

There are the snowdrops, their small, sharp leaves pricking up through the cold soil, dainty flowers shivering on thin stems. They may at first seem flowers of the winter, but they are the advance guard of spring, with the promise of reinforcements not far behind. The lacquered gold of winter aconites soon joins them; fat crocus buds steal up through the grass, and primroses start to put out tentative buds from their ruff of green foliage.

From then on, everything happens in a rush. Suddenly every plant is in a hurry, thrusting out new shoots. Swelling buds burst open; overnight, bare trees become clothed in a haze of pale green. The days lengthen noticeably, and some of them are soft and warm. Birds sing from dawn to dusk, voicing their relief that the harsh, hungry days of winter are behind them.

In the garden, it is the season of the bulb. With their store of food, they can afford to be the first to send up their blooms. Daffodils and narcissi, with flowers in every shade of yellow, cream and orange, are there from the earliest days of spring, when the tiny miniatures appear, to the latest, with the late, powerfully scented blooms of the old fashioned 'Pheasant's Eye'.

Most tulips are a little later on the scene than daffodils, though some of the species tulips are very early, and deserve to be more widely grown. Crocuses, hyacinths, grape hyacinths, irises and squills are soon all in full, heady bloom.

It is a busy season for the gardener. There is weeding to be done, digging to finish, sowings to be made. Lawns need their first cut of the year, and lawn edges may need straightening or repairing. Soon there are strong young stems to stake, feeding and dead-heading to be done, and as the early sowings germinate there is thinning and weeding of the seedlings to attend to. The greenhouse begins to fill with boxes of seedlings and young plants, and as the days grow warmer there are more and more plants to be sown outside, too.

Sometimes it is difficult to keep up with all the tasks that need doing in these busy spring days, but even so, gardeners should always make time to appreciate what is going on in the garden around them. Plants change so quickly in these hurried spring days that it is easy to miss them while they are at their brief moment of perfection. Spring blossoms may be spoiled by a shower or a cold wind and, in any case, their petals are quick to fall.

Late spring, almost-summer days are among the most pleasant of the year. Everything is still fresh and new, the weather is warm and gentle and the days long – and gardeners know there is a long and fruitful summer still to come.

# Early Spring

## FLOWERS AND ORNAMENTALS

**Prepare the soil for sowing annuals.** Annual beds can be very rewarding, but they must be started off well. The soil should be dug over thoroughly and all weeds and weed roots removed; if any well-rotted garden compost is available it should be added, particularly on very light, free-draining soil. The soil should be broken down into fine crumbs and then raked level just before sowing. An application of general fertilizer, raked into the surface, is a good idea.

If the soil is in good condition and the weather is kind, hardy annuals can be sown now. To make an annual bed, mark out patches for each type of flower with a trickle of silver sand. Within each patch, pull out short, shallow parallel drills in which to sow the seeds instead of scattering them at random. This makes it easy to distinguish between the annuals, which are in neat rows, and weed seedlings when they germinate.

Only hardy annuals can be sown this early. Anchusa, alyssum, calendula (pot marigold), candytuft, clarkia, echium, larkspur and nigella are among the most popular. Half-hardy annuals, such as erigeron, gaillardia, heliotrope, tagetes (French and African marigolds) and nicotiana must wait another few weeks until the weather is more reliable.

◀ The earliest flowers of spring are always among the most welcome in the garden. Here snowdrops, crocus and golden winter aconites are set off by the marbled foliage of hardy cyclamen.

**Weeds** are among the earliest plants to start growing. Remove weeds as soon as they are seen to keep on top of them – they can soon develop into a problem.

**Mulch perennial plants** with well-rotted compost or manure, particularly on free-draining soil. The soil should still be moist after the winter rains: a mulch now will help to keep that moisture there and prevent it evaporating. Heavy soils also benefit from mulching with organic matter, as it is eventually taken down into the soil, helping to lighten it and break it up.

**Plant snowdrops when they have finished flowering.** These bulbs transplant much more successfully when they are still in leaf than when they have died back to a dormant bulb. Plants are often available 'in the green' from specialist suppliers, and if you want to try some of the more choice varieties such as 'Sam Arnott' and 'Atkinsii', this is the best way to obtain them.

**Bare-root trees and shrubs can still be planted** but this should be finished as soon as possible, before they come into leaf. In a dry spring, newly planted subjects may well need watering.

**Sow sweet peas** in well-prepared soil outdoors. An attractive way to grow them is up wigwams of canes, rather like runner beans.

**Prune roses.** The next few weeks provide the best time to prune roses, when it is easy to see where the healthy buds are. Cut hybrid tea (large-flowered) varieties back hard, to within two or three buds of the base of the shoot. Cut just above a healthy, outward-facing bud. Floribunda (cluster-flowered) varieties are pruned a little less severely. As always, remove all dead, damaged or diseased wood first.

**Climbing plants on walls** can make a tangled mess of old and dead shoots after a few years' growth. Early spring is a good time to give

### · VEGETABLE SOWING ·

| Vegetable | Sow* | Harvest* |
|---|---|---|
| Bean, broad | Oct–Nov | May–June |
| | March–April | July–Sep |
| Bean, French | May | July–Sep |
| Bean, runner | April–May | July–Sep |
| Beetroot | March–July | June–Oct |
| Broccoli | April–May | Feb–April |
| Brussels sprout | March–April | Sep–March |
| Cabbage, summer | March–May | June–Sep |
| Cabbage, winter | April–June | Oct–April |
| Cabbage, spring | July–Aug | April–May |
| Carrot | March–June | June–March |
| Cauliflower | March–June | All year round |
| Celery | March–April | Aug–Nov |
| Courgette | March–May | July–Oct |
| Leek | March–April | Oct–March |
| Lettuce | March–Aug | May–Oct |
| Marrow | April–May | July–Oct |
| Onion | Feb–March | Aug–Oct |
| Onion, Japanese | Aug | June–July |
| Parsnip | March–April | Oct–March |
| Pea | March–June | June–Oct |
| | Oct–March | May–June |
| Radish | March–Sep | May–Oct |
| Radish, winter | Aug | Oct–March |
| Spinach | March–Aug | All year round |
| Swede | April–June | Sep–March |
| Sweet corn | April–May | Aug–Sep |
| Turnip | March–July | June–Oct |

*The months cited here are for the northern hemisphere. Southern hemisphere readers should refer to the table on page 6 for comparative timings.

vigorous types such as ivy an overhaul. Clip the shoots back close to the wall, then pull away some of the old growth to leave a framework of clinging branches spread out. Clear away dead leaves and the inevitable debris that accumulates in well-established plants. New spring growth will soon cover the wall again.

It is a good idea to provide a sturdy wooden framework for climbing plants to cling to. This should be fixed to the wall in such a way that it can be lowered, complete with clinging plants, when it is necessary to undertake any maintenance of the wall.

## VEGETABLES AND FRUIT

**Prepare the soil for making the first sowings of vegetables.** As for flowers, the soil must be well dug over, broken down to fine crumbs, and raked level to provide a seedbed.

The majority of vegetables are sown in mid-spring, but several can be sown now to provide a slightly earlier harvest. Carrots, peas, spinach, onions and broad beans are suitable, but choose those varieties marked as early in the seed catalogues. Make a small sowing only; save the main sowing for mid-spring when conditions are more reliable.

**Remove winter crops** that will be spoiled by starting into active growth again. Leeks need to be used up before they bolt, when the centre of the plant becomes a solid flower stem. Parsnips will start to sprout leaves from the crowns and eventually the roots will become flabby. Root crops can be lifted and stored in sand in a cool place to make them last a little longer. Brassicas, such as cabbages, kale, cauliflower and broccoli should still stand for some time, but keep an eye on them to ensure you use them before they are past their best.

# Sowing outdoors

Sowing outside must wait until the soil surface is dry enough to rake down to fine crumbs – not always easy to achieve in early spring. A few dry, sunny, breezy days are necessary on light, free-draining soil, but clay soils take longer to bring to the right condition. You must be able to walk on the soil without it clinging to your boots.

The soil should have been dug over in autumn and winter and the surface left rough for frosts to break down. Before sowing, the seedbed will need raking level, breaking down any clods with a sharp blow from the back of the rake. Once it is level, it is usually beneficial to shuffle over the seedbed to tread it firm, though this can be omitted on heavy soils. Then rake once again, using light strokes to bring the surface of the soil to fine crumbs.

Vegetables are normally sown in straight drills (shallow depressions in the soil). Use a garden line attached to two stakes to mark out a straight row, then pull a shallow, even drill along the line with the corner of a Dutch hoe (a). The depth depends on the size of the seed; 1–2 cm (½–¾ in) is normal.

Scatter the seed thinly along the drill (b), either by tapping it carefully out of the packet (having creased the edge to give a pouring lip) or by putting some seed into your hand and taking pinches of it.

Alternatively, seeds can be sown at 'stations'. If the plants are destined to end up 30 cm (12 in) apart, sow little groups of seed at the required spacing. This is more economical on seed, and makes thinning easier later.

Large seeds, such as runner beans, can be placed singly in the drill by hand, but sow a few extras at the ends of the row in case of failures. Beans and peas are usually sown in wide rows; for these it is easier to take out a wide, shallow drill with a spade.

Once the drill is sown, pull back the soil carefully with a rake to cover the seeds evenly (c), then tamp down the surface lightly. Don't forget to label the row.

Annual flowers are sown in patches marked out with sand. Draw small drills within each patch so the annuals germinate in straight rows, making it easier to identify weeds.

(a)  (b)  (c)

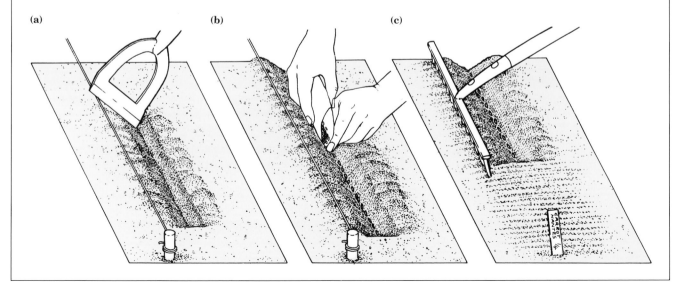

Plan for short-term garden features, such as a children's sand pit, to be replaced reasonably easily – perhaps by a pond – when it is no longer required.

**Plant early potatoes.** Choose a reasonably sheltered position for the first planting, and set the tubers 30 cm (12 in) apart in rows 75 cm (30 in) apart. Tubers should have been sprouted in a cool, light place, and the number of shoots reduced to the strongest two at an early stage; this gives a better overall yield than if a cluster of shoots is left.

**Plant rhubarb.** Rhubarb is a crop that is likely to stay in the same place for some years, so prepare the ground well, adding as much well-rotted compost or manure as possible. Plant the roots so that the crowns are level with the soil surface and firm in thoroughly.

Pull rhubarb sticks from forced plants as they become available.

**Winter spraying of fruit trees** used to be carried out with tar oil winter wash while the trees were fully dormant; tar oil would scorch any new growth and damage lawns beneath the trees. A liquid formulation of bromophos does the same job but can still be used in early spring, as it does not harm any buds which are bursting into growth. Overall insecticide spraying of fruit trees kills many overwintering pests, but also kills useful pest predators, so should not be carried out unless there is a particular and persistent problem.

**Protect early blossom on fruit trees** such as apricots and peaches. Net curtaining draped over the trees is usually sufficient to prevent them from being spoiled by frost.

# Garden planning

If you want to change your garden radically, or are starting from scratch, a proper plan will crystallize your thoughts and help avoid expensive mistakes.

The first step is to measure the garden accurately and sketch the basic shape to scale on graph paper. Add any trees, plants or other features you wish to keep. Next decide what type of garden you want. Should it be low maintenance? Is year-round interest important? Do you need a play area for children? Decide what you don't like about your present garden and see how you can improve it.

Think ahead to the future. Perhaps a pond is out of the question now because there are toddlers in the home, or maybe your present budget can't stretch to a conservatory – but things may be different in a few years' time. Don't construct expensive raised beds where a conservatory could go, but plan a patio there instead; give the toddlers a sand pit that can be replaced by a pond as they grow older.

Finally, with the help of a good nursery catalogue, select a range of plants that will complement the design and give you long-lasting pleasure.

**Make a scale plan of the outlines of the current garden (a), marking on it features that are to remain, such as trees and outbuildings. The proposed new plan can then be drawn (b), making it easier to convert to reality satisfactorily (c).**

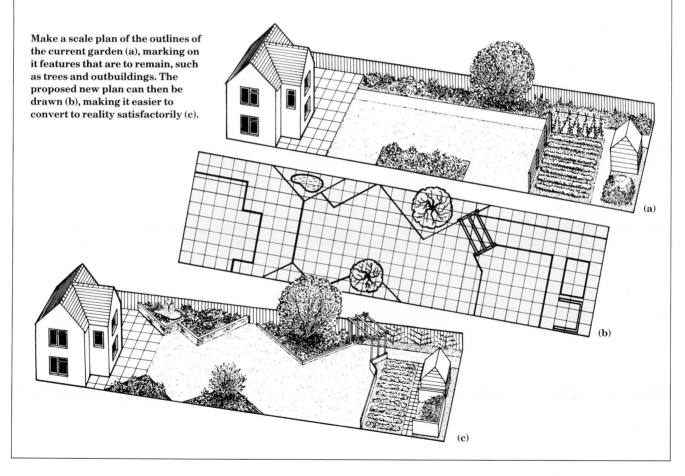

(a)

(b)

(c)

# A new lawn from seed

Grass seed can be sown in mid-spring or early autumn. Rotavate or dig the soil deeply and remove perennial weeds: incorporate a slow-acting fertilizer such as bonemeal. Tread or lightly roll the prepared soil to firm it, then break the surface down to fine crumbs, and rake it level. Water to moisten the soil thoroughly a day or two before sowing, if necessary.

Choose a lawn seed mixture to suit the situation (shady or sunny, for example) and the type of use your lawn will get.

Choose a dry, still day for sowing. Seed is usually applied at 50–65 g per sq m (1½–2 oz per sq yd) depending on the variety. Mark out a square metre or square yard with canes or string, weigh out the correct amount of seed and scatter it evenly over the marked out area so that you can see what the correct application rate looks like (see illustration). Then sow seed evenly over the whole lawn, sowing just beyond the proposed lawn edges. The sown area can be raked very lightly with a spring-tine rake to help cover some of the seeds.

Once the grass seedlings emerge (between one and three weeks after sowing) keep them moist, if necessary, by watering with a very fine spray. The new lawn can be mown when it reaches about 8 cm (3 in) high. The mower blades must be very sharp and set high, removing just the top 1 cm (½ in) of grass at the first cut and gradually lowered.

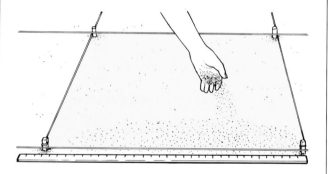

## HOUSE AND GREENHOUSE PLANTS

**Repot house plants** using a larger size pot if necessary. If the plants are to stay in the same size pot, remove some of the compost from around and on top of the root ball and replace it with fresh. Use a similar type of compost to that the plant is already growing in. Peat-based composts are popular because they are lightweight and clean and easy to handle, but because peat is a dwindling natural resource, alternatives such as coco fibre are being increasingly used.

**Increase watering** as house plants begin to grow more strongly. Keep the compost just moist at all times, not saturated. Begin feeding strong-growing plants with suitable liquid fertilizers.

**Clean greenhouse glass.** Over winter, grime and algae build up on the glass, reducing light transmission considerably. Clean the glass both outside and inside. If polythene double glazing is still in place, it is easier to leave cleaning the inside until this is taken down – generally once there is no longer any need to provide heat in the greenhouse. Even if double glazing is left in place all year round, it should be temporarily removed each spring to allow a thorough cleaning behind it.

**Ventilate the greenhouse** on sunny days, but remember to close up before nightfall.

**There are lots of sowings** to be made now, including half-hardy annuals and vegetables such as French and runner beans, tomatoes, melons and cucumbers.

**Prick off or pot up** sowings of tomatoes, melons and other crops made earlier.

**Take soft tip cuttings** of overwintered plants such as pelargoniums and fuchsias.

**Start tuberous-rooted begonias** into growth, setting the tubers dished side up in trays or pots of peat-based or similar compost.

# Mid-Spring

## FLOWERS AND ORNAMENTAL PLANTS

**Sow annuals.** Hardy annuals can still be sown, including some of the rather more delicate types such as star of the Veldt (*dimorphotheca*) and mesembryanthemums. In colder gardens it is usually better to sow now than in early spring. In sheltered places, half hardy annuals can also be sown outdoors soon, depending on the weather.

Thin hardy annuals sown earlier as soon as they begin to look crowded.

**Continue weeding and mulching** in flower and shrub borders. A good layer of mulching material on weed-free soil will help to prevent new weeds appearing, as well as conserving soil moisture.

**Divide border plants.** This job is often done in autumn, but spring is also a suitable time. Do not leave it much later than this, or the plants will be growing strongly and will receive a check when replanted.

**Plant alpines.** They will usually establish readily at this time of year. When planting rock gardens it is often difficult to fit the root ball of container-grown plants into cracks and crevices. If necessary the soil can be washed off the roots carefully until they can be fitted into the planting space, but try to avoid damaging the roots. Buy small plants to fit into tiny spaces, and ensure they have some good soil round their roots when planted.

**Plant bare-root evergreen shrubs.** Autumn and winter are the seasons for planting deciduous bare-root subjects, but evergreens prefer mid spring. It is often necessary to protect newly

## Weeding

A weed is any plant growing where it is not wanted, and where it competes with cultivated plants for light, moisture, nutrients and space.

Weeds can be divided into two main groups: annual and perennial. Annual weeds only survive for a season, but they seed very freely, ensuring problems for future years. Perennial weeds can survive for many years, often persisting underground as a strong rootstock.

Golden rules when dealing with weeds are:
- Remove all traces of perennial weed roots when preparing new ground or during winter digging.
- Remove weed seedlings and young plants quickly.
- Do not allow annual weeds to go to seed.
- Do not put perennial weed roots, or weed seedheads, on the compost heap.

Combat weeds by hoeing (a), using a sharp hoe to slice young plants off at soil level (best on a dry day); deep mulching, to smother weed seedling growth; and, if necessary, by the careful use of suitable herbicides (b).

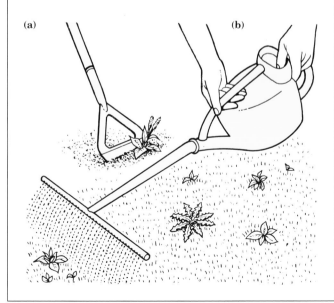

(a)　　　　(b)

15

◄ The honey-scented flowers of *Buddleia davidii* may be white as well as the more familiar purple shades; all varieties seem to be equally attractive to butterflies such as these small tortoiseshells.

► Bedding plants should be thoroughly hardened off, preferably in a cold frame, before they are planted out in their flowering positions.

planted subjects from the prevailing wind, as this can scorch the foliage; conifers are frequently badly affected. Make a temporary screen from sacking (hessian or plastic) firmly supported on stout posts. Don't forget to water the plants if the weather is dry.

**Prune butterfly bush** (*Buddleia davidii*). Pruning of this shrub is often neglected, with straggly, ungainly results. It benefits from being pruned very hard, to within 30 cm (1 ft) or so of the ground. A saw is usually necessary to do the job properly. Vigorous new growth soon shoots from the old wood and will produce plenty of good quality flowers.

If you prefer a larger, tree shape, build up a framework of three or four main branches care-fully, selecting those that are in the best positions, then cut back to within 30 cm (1 ft) or so of this framework each year.

**Bedding plants** appear in the garden centres and shops earlier each year. It is still too early to plant out summer bedding, so if you buy plants, keep them in a cold frame or unheated, well-ventilated greenhouse, gradually hardening them off. Choose small but sturdy, healthy plants.

**Containerized shrubs and roses** can be a bad buy at this time of year – they may have been only recently lifted from open ground and potted up. If you are suspicious, try knocking the plant out of its pot. A container-grown plant will turn out with root ball intact; a newly potted plant will be easy to spot.

# Mowing lawns

Correct mowing of lawns is necessary both to give them an attractive appearance and keep lawn weeds under control. Grass thrives on regular mowing, but it will kill many broad-leaved weeds, though others have managed to adapt.

How you mow your lawn depends on the uses to which it will be put. Turf which has to work hard for its living – providing a football pitch for enthusiastic youngsters, for example – should not be mown as closely as a purely ornamental lawn.

There is a wide choice of mowers, ranging from simple hand mowers to those trailed behind a tractor. The first choice you are likely to have to make is between a cylinder mower (a) (where a set of turning blades meets a fixed bottom blade and cuts the grass with a scissor action) and a rotary mower (b) (where the blade rotates horizontally at high speed). Most cylinder mowers have a rear roller which gives the lawn attractive stripes, though an increasing number of rotary mowers are now fitted with these. Cylinder mowers tend to give the highest quality cut and are generally used on the finest lawns, though for most gardeners with a utility lawn a good rotary mower will give equally acceptable results. For areas of rough grass, or on sloping banks, a rotary is far easier to use.

Mowing should take place regularly throughout the growing season, and may be necessary occasionally during mild spells in winter. Before mowing, remove stones from the lawn surface to avoid damage to the mower and operator. The grass should preferably be dry. At intervals throughout the season check that the blades are correctly adjusted – and sharp.

In spring and autumn, mow once a week; in summer increase this to twice a week unless the weather is very dry. For a utility lawn, the height of cut should be not less than 2 cm (¾ in) in summer, and 3–4 cm (1–1½ in) in spring and autumn .

Luxury, ornamental lawns can be cut a little closer, but they should never be cut below 0.5 cm (¼ in). If the grass has grown longer than you would like, do not mow it to the correct height straight away, but tip it back gradually over a couple of weeks.

Vary the direction each time you cut – in other words, alternate between mowing east/west and north/south. This helps prevent ridges appearing.

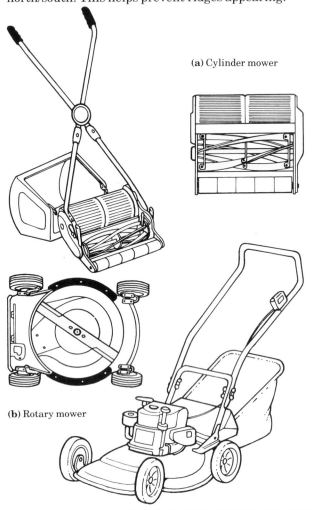

(a) Cylinder mower

(b) Rotary mower

## LAWNS

**Mowing of lawns starts now** and will be a regular job for the rest of the growing season. Do not make the first cut too low; tip the grass lightly and gradually lower the blades (see page 18).

**If you are sowing a new lawn** choose the type of seed carefully. It should be suitable for both the type of use the lawn is going to get, and the situation (see page 14).

For a utility but still ornamental lawn, you could try one of the newer, fine-leaved, hard-wearing rye grasses.

## FRUIT AND VEGETABLES

**Continue sowing vegetable seeds** for a succession of crops. Sow short rows of vegetables such as lettuce, so that you do not have too many maturing all at once.

**Sow winter brassicas** such as cabbages, Brussels sprouts, kale and sprouting broccoli. These are sown in a seedbed for transplanting later. Sow thinly in short rows and remember to label each row clearly – one brassica seedling looks very much like another. Brassica plants can be bought from garden centres and market stalls quite cheaply for planting out later; this may save the trouble of raising them from seed, but there is a real risk of introducing club root disease to the garden on the roots of bought-in plants. Once this disease is in the soil it is there for good, so it pays to take a little trouble to keep it out. Besides which, growing from seed enables you to have a much better choice of varieties.

**Thin out vegetable seedlings** sown earlier. Don't wait until the plants are overcrowded in the rows, but thin them early, leaving the strongest. Always try to sow thinly to minimize the thinning that is required later, particularly with carrots. The scent of the bruised foliage attracts carrot root flies to lay their eggs, so the less handling of the plants that takes place, the better.

**Salad vegetables** are some of the best crops to grow at home, where just-picked freshness is of real importance. There are many different sorts to grow, and there is a huge choice of varieties even for a basic like lettuce – from old favourites like crisp 'Webbs Wonderful' to the compact Cos 'Little Gem', frilly edged 'Lollo Rosso', oak-leaved red and green 'Salad Bowl' and, of course, the familar butterhead or cabbage lettuce such as 'Tom Thumb'. Lamb's lettuce is a soft-leaved tender plant for both summer and winter salads; purslane has succulent leaves with a spicy 'bite'. They are all easy to grow, and should be sown little and often.

**Plant out leeks** which have been raised in a frame or greenhouse and hardened off. Separate the leek seedlings and put them in neat bundles with the bases of the seedlings together. With sharp scissors, cut off the tips of the leaves ('flags') and reduce the roots to about 1 cm (½ in): each seedling should be 13–15 cm (5–6 in) long overall. This seems drastic treatment, but it makes planting a lot easier, and the leeks thrive on it. Make deep holes with a large dibber and drop a leek in each hole so the tips of the flags are showing above the surface. Water with a can to wash a little soil down over the roots of the seedlings, but do not fill the holes with soil. This planting method really works.

## GREENHOUSE AND HOUSE PLANTS

**Pests thrive as the days get warmer**, as do plants. Be on the look out for the first signs of greenfly (aphid) infestation, particularly on tender young growing tips and on the undersides of leaves.

◄ Lettuce is a staple for summer salads, but you don't have to grow familiar, boring varieties. The deep red-coloured, oak-leaved 'Red Salad Bowl' is both tasty and attractive in growth.

► Paint-on whitewash is one of the cheapest methods of shading a greenhouse. At the end of the season, the shading can be removed by rubbing it off with a dry cloth.

**Increase greenhouse ventilation** as the weather improves, using side vents as well as roof vents. Automatic ventilators, which adjust themselves according to temperature, are ideal for spring and autumn days, when the weather can be difficult to predict.

**Prick out seedlings** as soon as they can be handled easily and before they become overcrowded. More and more space is needed as boxes of seedlings are pricked out. A garden frame is of double benefit now, making it easy to harden plants off gradually before they are planted outside, and increasing the room in the greenhouse at the same time. Purpose-built aluminium or wooden frames can be bought, or one can be knocked up easily and cheaply with a few bricks or planks for the frame, and an old window from a demolition yard for the light. Make sure you can ventilate the frame without too much trouble.

**Apply shading to greenhouses** as soon as necessary. Use paint-on whitewash or netting. It is worth shading at least part of the greenhouse now to protect delicate seedlings from direct sun.

**Plant tomatoes** in heated greenhouses. Growing bags give good results but need frequent watering; plants are less likely to suffer water stress if they are planted direct in the greenhouse border.

**Harden off bedding plants** ready to plant out when all danger of frost is past.

**Take chrysanthemum cuttings** from overwintered roots. Insert them in sandy compost and keep them just moist.

# Late Spring

## FLOWERS AND ORNAMENTALS

**Thin hardy annuals** sown earlier. Thin them out in two or three stages until they reach an eventual spacing of 20–45 cm (8–18 in) depending on the type of plant. If sown in straight drills, it will be easy to identify them and remove weed seedlings.

**Check herbaceous perennials for pests,** particularly slugs and snails, which love the soft young shoots. Certain plants seem to be irresistible to them – hosta leaves are frequently reduced to skeletons even before they unfold. Susceptible plants can be protected with slug pellets, but these must be hidden under a propped-up tile or plant pot to try to prevent hedgehogs, birds and other wildlife being poisoned by them.

**Feed border plants, trees and shrubs.** An application of general fertilizer for leafy plants, and high-potash fertilizer for flowering plants, will help plants to sustain the spurt of growth they are making now.

**Stake perennial plants early**, so that the plants can grow through the supports naturally – it is always difficult to disguise stakes if they are put in later. For reasonably compact plants, twiggy pea sticks make good, natural-looking supports. Sturdy wooden stakes, bamboo or plastic canes and string can be used to support individual taller stems, or proprietary interlocking wire stakes can inconspicuously encircle entire clumps. There are also supports formed from a circle of wire mesh on tall legs: they only need to be placed over the plant, pushing the legs firmly into the soil, and the stems gently guided through the mesh as they grow.

Remember that border plants should be allowed to form a gentle, loose shape, with support where necessary, for single stems. They shouldn't be bunched up and trussed with a tight loop of string to a single cane.

| · WINDOW BOXES AND HANGING BASKETS · | |
| --- | --- |
| **Trailing plants** | **Description** |
| Fuchsia | Bell-like flowers in a range of red, purple and white shades; make sure you choose the correct variety – not all are trailing. |
| *Glechoma hederacea* | Serrated, rounded, green leaves edged with white. |
| *Helichrysum petiolare* | Silvery green, velvety foliage; 'Limelight' is golden; there is also a variegated variety. |
| *Hedera helix* | Ivies are available in a good range of colours, leaf shapes and variegation. |
| Lobelia | Cascades of blue flowers; now also available in red shades. |
| *Lysimachia nummularia* | Cascading pale green foliage, golden in the variety 'Aurea'. |
| Nasturtium | Attractive rounded leaves and flowers in brilliant orange shades. |
| Pelargonium (ivy-leaved) | These varieties have masses of pink, red, white or salmon flowers on long, trailing stems. |
| **Upright plants** | **Description** |
| Begonia | Tuberous varieties have large, often fully double flowers in a range of bright colours: semperflorens types have smaller, single blooms, very freely produced. |
| Fuchsia | Bush varieties make good centrepieces. They may need staking. |
| Marguerite | Divided foliage and copious daisy-like flowers; suitable for larger containers. |
| Pelargonium | Shrubby, stocky plants with a good flower colour range. |

**Plant up windowboxes and hanging baskets** (see illustration). Use a good selection of trailing and upright plants – see chart opposite for some suggestions.

**Keep beds and borders weed free** as far as possible. Take care when hoeing close to plants – it is all too easy to damage them.

**Check roses for disease** such as blackspot. Fungus diseases occur in warm, wet weather, and though summer is the usual time to spot them, they can start much earlier. If disease has been a problem in previous years, spray with preventive fungicide as soon as the leaves start to open.

**Continue sowing hardy and half-hardy annuals** where they are to flower.

**Plant stored dahlia tubers.** These can safely be planted outside now, covering the crowns with about 8 cm (3 in) of soil to protect the shoots against any late frosts.

**Most daffodils and narcissi are now past their best,** but the bulbs need to build up their reserves for flowering next year. Do not cut off or tie up the leaves or you will prevent this process. The foliage should be left alone for six weeks after the flowers fade. If you want to clear a bed or border to plant summer bedding, lift the bulbs carefully and heel them in (replant them shallowly) in a spare piece of ground to continue ripening. When naturalizing bulbs in grass, remember that you will not be able to mow the grass for a long time.

**Trailing laburnum flowers** are one of the most beautiful sights of this time of year, with small trees weighed down under the graceful racemes of yellow blooms. All parts of this attractive tree are poisonous, and great care must be taken where young children might have access to it. The most dangerous parts are the seeds; the bean-like seed pod has encouraged children to sample the contents. Cutting off the faded flowers before the

Planting a hanging basket is made much easier if it is supported in a large pot or similar. Water thoroughly immediately planting is complete.

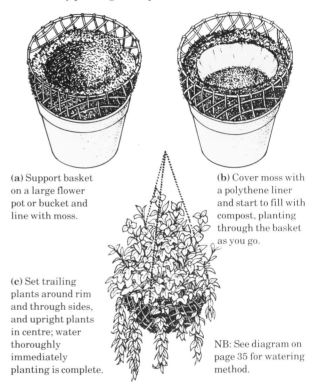

(a) Support basket on a large flower pot or bucket and line with moss.

(b) Cover moss with a polythene liner and start to fill with compost, planting through the basket as you go.

(c) Set trailing plants around rim and through sides, and upright plants in centre; water thoroughly immediately planting is complete.

NB: See diagram on page 35 for watering method.

pods form is one way of avoiding danger. The hybrid *Laburnum × watereri* 'Vossii' tends to set few seeds, making it a good choice for gardens with children – but it is a beautiful form in any case, worth choosing for its long racemes of flowers alone.

**Plant out summer bedding.** As long as the plants are thoroughly hardened off it should now be safe to plant them out in most gardens, though if you are in a particularly cold area or a frost pocket you will still need to take care. The more exotic plants such as cannas should be left until early summer to be on the safe side.

23

## LAWNS

**Mow lawns as frequently as necessary.** This will depend mainly on the amount of rain that falls, but the grass should be mown regularly so that it only needs tipping back each time. The length at which it is kept depends on the uses to which it is put (see page 18).

**Lawn weeds** are usually growing as fast or faster than the grass at this time of year, making it an excellent time to treat them. Various selective weedkillers are available which will kill broad-leaved weeds without harming the grass – as long as they are applied correctly. Always follow the instructions on the pack very carefully. Selective hormone weedkillers can be carried considerable distances on the slightest breeze to cause characteristic damage to sensitive plants such as tomatoes and vines. Always choose a still day for application.

## WATER GARDENS

**Plant all types of pond plants.** This is the ideal time of year for making or renovating a garden pond, or introducing new plants. Always use fertile garden soil or a loam-based compost in planting baskets – lightweight peat composts will tend to float away. Top off the basket with coarse gravel to keep the soil in place.

**Thin out overgrown plants.** Oxygenators can sometimes crowd out a pond, and can be thinned out now if necessary, but remember that healthy growth of oxygenators is essential to keep the water in good condition. Water-lilies and other submerged plants that have outgrown their baskets can be lifted and cut into smaller crowns with a sharp knife before being replanted. Many popular water-lily varieties are too vigorous for small ponds. Think about buying a new, compact variety if your lily regularly outgrows its welcome. 'James Brydon' is one of the best varieties, small to medium in size, with deep rosy red flowers, freely produced.

**Aphids can often be found on water-lily leaves.** Deal with them by submerging the leaves for a few seconds. The water will carry the greenfly away and any fish in the pond will soon make short work of them! Release the leaves and they will spring back to the surface.

◀ The trailing racemes of golden laburnum flowers are outstandingly beautiful, but all parts of the tree are poisonous, particularly the seeds.

▶ The serene and restful air of a water feature is an asset in any garden. Early summer is the best time for planting pond plants and introducing fish.

**Feed fish** small amounts of floating fish food, clearing up any that remains uneaten after a few minutes. A well-stocked pond contains plenty of natural food at this time of year, and if the fish don't seem interested in your offerings, forget about feeding until later in the summer.

## VEGETABLES AND FRUIT

**Sow runner beans outdoors.** It should now be safe to sow these in all areas. Always sow a few extra at the ends of the rows so that you have spare plants in case any seeds in the row fail to germinate.

**Other tender vegetables** can also be sown safely outdoors now, including sweet corn, marrows, courgettes and cucumbers. If you have a greenhouse or frame so that you can raise plants earlier, so much the better, but good results can still be had from an outdoor sowing.

**Plant pot-grown beans, marrows, cucumbers and outdoor tomatoes** once they have been sufficiently hardened off and you are sure all danger of frost is past.

**Sow Chinese cabbage.** This crop is useful both for salads and as a cooked vegetable. It must be sown where it is to grow, as it will run to seed if transplanted.

**Earth up early potatoes** as the shoots come through the soil.

**Stake peas** with twiggy sticks as they grow. All varieties, even the dwarf ones, need support if the peas are to be easy to pick.

**Continue thinning seedlings** as necessary, and continue to make successional sowings for extended cropping.

**Remove weeds at an early stage**, as they compete with crops for both water and nutrients. Hoeing is the quickest way to deal with weeds between the rows. Make sure the hoe blade is

# Making a water garden

A water feature adds a new dimension to any garden, particularly if moving water is involved. The most popular water feature is a pond, which is not too difficult to construct.

Basic points to bear in mind are:
- Make the pond as large as possible – it will be much easier to look after.
- Simple, flowing shapes are most effective.
- Site the pond in full sun, away from trees.
- Ensure it has enough depth to stop the water freezing solid in winter – a minimum of 60 cm (2 ft). Moulded fibre glass ponds are a popular option, but for maximum flexibility and long life, a butyl rubber liner is hard to beat. Once the pond is complete, plant it up with oxygenators such as *Elodea canadensis* (these are vital to keep the water clear) and a range of floating and marginal plants. Fish can be introduced once the plants are established.

The water in any new pond will fill with algae within a few days, turning bright green or even red. This is an essential part of the establishment process and will gradually clear. Changing the water will only prolong the process.

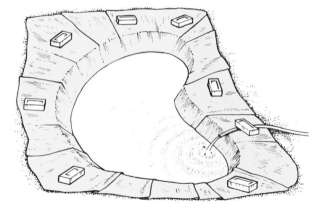

When filling a new pond, hold the liner in position with bricks while gently running the water in. Adjust the bricks as necessary as the pond fills.

sharp and the weeds are small for the best results. Mulching helps prevent weeds and reduces water loss, and planting through a black plastic sheet, well buried at the edges, is a good labour-saving idea.

**Asparagus beds** now start to produce their welcome, short-lived harvest of spears. Cut each spear as soon as it is large enough to eat, cutting just below ground level with a sharp knife and being careful not to damage other spears that may be just about to emerge. Check the bed frequently, especially in hot weather. The spears grow very rapidly, and once the bud scales start to open out they are nowhere near as good to eat. Cutting can continue for about six weeks, then leave the plants to develop their ferns. Extending the season will only spoil future crops.

**Plant out winter brassicas.** Water the area where they are to be planted the evening before. Make planting holes with a dibber or trowel and firm the plants very thoroughly, treading the soil around them with your foot. Try pulling at a leaf to see if they are firm enough – the leaf should tear before the plant lifts. Plenty of water will be needed after planting, especially if it's sunny.

**Straw down strawberry beds.** Place clean straw along the rows, tucking it well underneath the plants. This keeps the developing fruit clean and dry and away from slugs. Black plastic can be used instead, but is not quite as effective.

Do not straw down the beds while there is still risk of night frosts; bare soil gives off warmth which helps to protect the flowers from frost damage. Flowers which have been frosted can easily be spotted by their blackened central eye.

## GREENHOUSE AND HOUSE PLANTS

**Pot up rooted cuttings.** It is generally obvious when cuttings are well rooted by the fresh 'growy' look to the tips of the shoots, which look rather dull before rooting has taken place. Lever the plants out of their compost carefully with a dibber or forked stick, to avoid damaging the new roots as much as possible. Pot them up individually and firm them in lightly.

**Pinch out the growing tips** of plants such as pelargoniums and fuchsias in order to make them bushy and compact.

**Keep checking for pests** regularly and treating them as soon as they are found. This does not have to mean using chemicals – prompt removal of an infested leaf may be all that is required to prevent the problem spreading.

**Apply shading to greenhouses** if this has not already been done. The temperature in unshaded houses rises rapidly in sunshine, and foliage can be scorched through the glass.

**Train cucumbers and tomatoes** growing in heated greenhouses. Tomatoes should be supported by a stake or wound round twine attached to the greenhouse roof. Side shoots should be removed while they are still small. Cucumbers are trained up a wire or twine until the main stem reaches the ridge of the greenhouse, when it is pinched out. Side shoots are pinched out once they carry two fruits, and any further shoots that develop from side shoots are pinched out at the first pair of leaves. Remove male flowers to prevent them pollinating the female flowers, or bitter, misshapen fruits will be produced.

**Melons** are grown in a similar way to cucumbers, but in this case flowers need to be pollinated to produce fruits. Hand pollination is advisable for a good set. Female fruits can be identified by the small swelling immediately behind the flower.

**Cyclamen should be allowed to rest** until late summer. Stop watering the plants and remove leaves as they die back. Turn the pots on their sides under the greenhouse bench.

◄ Damping down the greenhouse floor and staging lowers the temperature and increases the humidity, and should be carried out more frequently as the weather gets warmer.

► Continental-style pelargoniums make an eye-catching windowbox when they are well grown. They need a good summer, with plenty of sun, and careful feeding once they are established.

**House plants like jasmine and Christmas cherry** can be put outside in a sheltered spot for the summer. This helps to ripen the wood to ensure a good show of flowers and fruit next year.

**Continental pelargoniums** are always admired spilling over the windowboxes of chocolate-box Swiss chalets in a waterfall of colour. These plants need a good summer with plenty of sun to perform well, but they are stunning when they do. Called 'Balcon' pelargoniums, they are available in a range of pink and red shades. It is important not to feed the plants too soon, but to wait until they have made vigorous, branching plants before giving them their first high-potash liquid feed. Feeding should then continue every 10 days through the summer. Plants are available from pelargonium specialists.

**Damping down** of the greenhouse floor and staging to lower the temperature and increase humidity can be done on very hot, sunny days. Avoid a damp atmosphere in the cool of evening, or you will encourage fungus diseases.

**Automatic greenhouse watering systems** are a boon for a busy or often-absent gardener, but frequent checks are still needed to ensure each plant is receiving the right amount of water for its needs.

If you can't afford a fully-automated watering system, a seep hose is an easy and efficient way of watering plants in the greenhouse border.

# · 2 ·
# Summer

Summer is the time when we can enjoy the garden to the full. Not only is the weather generally warm and pleasant enough to make being outside enjoyable, but plants are at their best, too. In early summer, growth is fresh and luxuriant; flowers begin to fill the borders with colour and scent and the grass grows lush and green. Trees, while in full leaf, retain their spring brightness and lightness; the air is filled with bird song. Growth is amazingly rapid as the warmth and still-present moisture of spring rains provide perfect conditions for plants: wild flowers and weeds, however, grow as fast (often much faster, it seems) than the cultivated plants in our gardens. As the plants put out their succulent new shoots, so the sap-sucking insects get to work, too. Hordes of aphids appear overnight on the tips of broad bean plants, and cluster thickly round the rose buds. But generally, hot on their heels comes an army of ladybirds to munch their way through the pests, reducing them to something more like acceptable levels.

As the summer progresses, rain becomes insufficient to sustain that rapid spurt of growth of the early season, and things slow down. Days are long and often hot. Birds stop singing and begin to skulk in hedgerows and among bushes, sheltering from the sun. Lawns begin to lose their emerald tones; leaves on the heavily clothed trees start to look a little dull and lacklustre.

Flowers, however, are in full, heady bloom, and the drone of bees working them for nectar is a lazy background note to the mid-summer days. Weeds run quickly to flower, too, and shed their thousands of seeds far and wide to lie dormant in the soil and provide new populations for years to come.

Although there may be rainy days, the weather is often very dry. Summer showers provide the earthy scent of rain falling on the dry, dusty soil: as far as many gardeners are concerned, it's a welcome scent to rival that of the most heavily perfumed flower. This is the time when any steps that have been taken to improve the soil texture and water-holding capacity pay handsome dividends, improving plant growth and cutting down on the amount of watering needed.

Late summer is a time of heat and thunderstorms, with torrential rains sometimes beating stems to the ground, but helping to replenish soil moisture, and restoring straw-coloured lawns to greenness. Fruit and vegetables start to mature rapidly, keeping the kitchen gardener busy. Flowers are still making a colourful spectacle in the garden but are not now being produced with quite such abundance; some of the late season species such as heleniums, achillea and dahlias are in full bloom, and Michaelmas daisies and chrysanthemums are ready to make their appearance, reminding us that autumn is on the way.

# Watering

During hot, dry summer months it is often necessary to water plants to keep them growing well. In periods of drought water is a limited resource, so we must learn to use it wisely.

Plants draw water from the soil through their roots, and it travels upward to all parts of the plant and eventually evaporates from the leaf surfaces. When water is in short supply, plant growth will be slowed: eventually, when more water is being lost from the foliage than can be replaced from the soil, plants will wilt and may die. Very hot, sunny days obviously increase the amount of water lost from the foliage, but dry, windy days also have the same effect.

First step in avoiding water stress is to increase the water-holding capacity of the soil. This is particularly important on light, sandy soils, where rain water quickly drains away. Heavy applications of bulky organic matter – well-rotted manure or garden compost – act as a sponge to soak up and hold on to water against times of shortage.

When the soil is moist, at the beginning of the season, help prevent that moisture being lost through the summer by mulching. A good depth of compost, manure, bark chips, or even a sheet of plastic (dug in round the edges and disguised with a covering of shredded bark) can all be used.

Young and newly transplanted plants are the first to suffer from lack of water, and these should receive the first attention when watering is necessary. It is important to water thoroughly. Just dampening the soil surface encourages roots to grow in the top layer of soil where they will be even more prone to drying out in future. Ensure the soil is moist in the root area of the plants.

Because surprisingly large amounts of water are necessary to achieve this, watering with a hose is more successful than with a watering can. A seep hose – a piece of hose with small holes along its length, through which water gradually seeps out – can be left in place among plants for several hours, and little water is lost by evaporation. Sprinklers are also easy to use, but the droplets can damage plants if you are not careful in setting them up. In periods of drought, remember that the use of hoses and sprinklers may be banned.

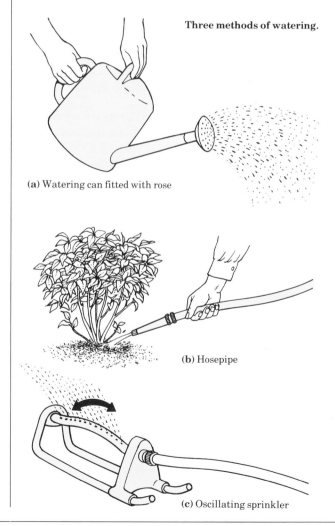

**Three methods of watering.**

(a) Watering can fitted with rose

(b) Hosepipe

(c) Oscillating sprinkler

# Early Summer

## FLOWERS AND ORNAMENTALS

**Stake and tie in plants as they grow.** Once stems flop it is very difficult to make them into a shapely plant again. The tips of blooms such as those of delphiniums and lupins will continue to grow straight up even if the stems are lying flat on the soil, so unless stems are picked up immediately they fall, a permanently misshapen flower spike will be the result.

**Pests are on the increase now,** as there is plenty of luscious new growth for them to feed on. Check plants regularly, particularly around flower buds, where aphids tend to congregate. Prompt treatment of a small infestation will help prevent it developing into a full-scale attack.

Sometimes pests can be very simply treated by washing them off with the jet from a hose or rubbing them off with your fingers. Where there are too many to make this effective, use a suitable pesticide. Do take care to avoid damage to pollinating insects like bees by not spraying open flowers with insecticides.

**Water plants where necessary** if sufficient rain does not fall. Give enough water to penetrate to the roots, not just wet the soil surface. Newly planted specimens are the most likely to suffer; well-established plants are less likely to need supplementary watering.

**Sow biennials and perennials in a seedbed.** A small corner of the vegetable plot is often used for this. Sow seed thinly in short drills about 30 cm (1 ft) apart; if the soil is very dry, water the base of the drills before sowing. Wallflowers, sweet Williams and forget-me-nots are popular subjects.

**Increase border pinks from pipings.** These are a form of cutting, and are taken by pulling a healthy, leafy stem about 10 cm (4 in) long from a

Borders filled with colourful summer blooms are set off to perfection by a well-maintained lawn.

A trellis draped with climbing plants greatly enhances the patio area, as well as providing it with shelter and privacy.

# Garden living space

Increasing numbers of people are treating the garden as an extension of the house – an outdoor room in which to eat, relax and generally enjoy life in the summer months.

The part of the garden which is most likely to be used is that which adjoins the house, so that it is easy to slip inside to fetch a drink, or attend to the cooking. Patio doors are the most popular link between the garden and house; on older, traditional style properties, French windows may be more appropriate. Immediately outside the doors, a patio – generally simply a paved area – provides a firm surface for all weathers.

In areas where the weather is not always warm, some form of shelter for the patio area will extend its use. A trellis clothed with climbing plants, protecting against the prevailing wind, can be a very attractive solution.

Garden furniture can range from simple wooden deckchairs to luxuriously upholstered loungers, but furniture that can be left outside all summer is likely to prove the most popular. Treated wood, cast aluminium or plastic are all suitable. A barbecue can be built in to the patio wall, and outdoor lighting means the garden can be enjoyed late into the evening after a warm summer day.

joint. It should come out easily. Insert these firmly in sandy soil in a shady place and keep them moist.

**Continue feeding plants** for strong growth, but don't apply powder or granule fertilizers in very dry conditions or they could scorch roots. If it does not rain, water in any fertilizer applications copiously. Normal strength liquid feeds can be applied without harm.

**Trim evergreen hedges.** Hedge cutting is never a popular job, but power hedge trimmers take a lot of the pain out of it. Remember that they are potentially very dangerous. Not only are the blades sharp, but an electric trimmer has the

---

· USING CHEMICALS IN THE GARDEN ·

With all fruit spraying, take great care to avoid damage to pollinating insects.

- Use the correct chemicals and apply them strictly according to the directions on the label.

- Always choose the least persistent chemical available.

- Do not spray fruit while the flowers are open. This is particularly important with raspberries, which are very attractive to bees. Wait until the petals on all the flowers are falling.

- Spray in the evening, when most pollinating insects have stopped flying.

- Dispose of surplus spray solution by pouring it on to clean soil. Do not pour it down the drains, or leave it in the sprayer for use later. Make up the minimum amount of solution necessary.

- Store all chemicals in a safe place, preferably in a locked cabinet.

- If you lose the instructions for a particular product, or the label has become illegible, do not use it, but dispose of it safely (ask your local council for advice on disposal facilities).

---

added risk of electrocution. Any hedge above waist height means extra danger because of manipulating the trimmer in awkward positions. Always remember these safety points:

- Keep your power trimmer well maintained and serviced.
- For electric trimmers, use an earth leakage circuit breaker at the socket.
- Work with the electric cable over your shoulder, out of the way of the blades. Special cable harnesses are available.
- Don't work with a hedge trimmer above your head.
- When using steps, ensure they are firm and stable. Don't lean a ladder into a hedge – it may not support the weight.

Cut hedges into a broad wedge shape, with the widest part of the wedge at the base.

**Divide crowded flag irises** that have finished flowering. Prise the rhizomes up with a fork and cut them into sections about 10 cm (4 in) long, each with a fan of leaves attached. Use only healthy young growth; the old, central part of the rhizome that bears no foliage can be discarded. Replant the sections of rhizome shallowly, only just covering them with soil to hold them in place. This job generally needs doing every few years, and rejuvenates the plants.

**Prune spring-flowering shrubs.** These should be pruned straight after flowering (if any pruning is necessary), giving them time to make new growth for flowering next year. Cut them back just enough to give a well-balanced shape and keep them in bounds.

Remove faded flowers on rhododendrons and azaleas, brooms and lilacs to keep them looking good.

**Feed and water plants in containers regularly.** They may need twice-daily watering in dry weather.

# Plants in containers

Summer bedding plants make an excellent display when grown in containers such as window boxes, hanging baskets and tubs. They can be used to brighten up all sorts of areas where it is impossible to grow plants in the ground: even houses without gardens can become a blaze of colour from flowers!

Plants grown in containers need special care. For the best effect, they should be very closely planted, packing as many plants as possible in to the space available. This means that the relatively small amount of soil in the container is soon filled with roots, and moisture and plant nutrients are quickly used up. Drainage needs to be good, however, for the soil can also become waterlogged very easily.

### Tubs and window boxes

Choose as large a style as practical, and make sure the base has adequate drainage holes. If necessary, drill extra holes yourself. If this is impossible, you will have to rely on good crocking for drainage. This means putting a layer of coarse rubble (broken clay plant pots are ideal) in the base of the container to provide a space for water to drain. Even where

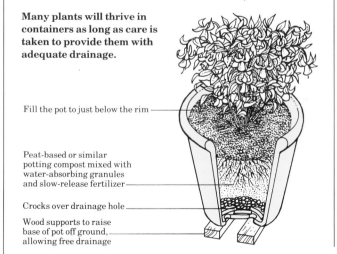

**Many plants will thrive in containers as long as care is taken to provide them with adequate drainage.**

Fill the pot to just below the rim

Peat-based or similar potting compost mixed with water-absorbing granules and slow-release fertilizer

Crocks over drainage hole

Wood supports to raise base of pot off ground, allowing free drainage

**Watering hanging baskets can be awkward, but is made much easier by sinking a small pot in the compost and filling this at each watering.**

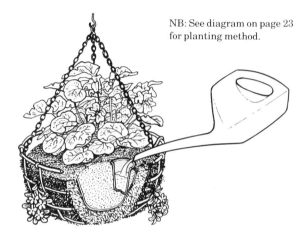

NB: See diagram on page 23 for planting method.

drainage holes exist, crock over the top of them to make sure they do not become blocked by compost. Stand the container on blocks of wood or bricks to raise the base off the ground (see left).

Fill with good quality potting compost. Lightweight peat-based (or peat substitute) composts are best for window boxes, and tubs which will need to be moved. Mix in water-absorbing granules to improve the compost's water-holding capacity, and a slow-release fertilizer.

### Hanging baskets

Line the basket with a good thickness of moss, then fill with compost mix as above. Water-absorbing granules are even more important for hanging baskets. A small clay plant pot should be buried to its rim in the compost towards the edge of the basket, to be filled up when watering (see above).

All containers must be watered daily or twice daily in sunny weather, and a liquid fertilizer applied twice a week to mature plants.

**Cut back spring-flowering wall plants** such as iberis and aubrieta. A pair of shears can be used to give them a haircut and keep them tidy and in good shape for next spring.

**Divide primulas,** including auriculas, and replant in moist soil.

## LAWNS

**Lawns need regular mowing** before grass gets too long. Feeding and weedkilling can also be carried out now. If the weather has been dry, a thorough watering will keep the grass green – as long as watering is not restricted due to drought.

## VEGETABLES AND FRUIT

**Continue weeding regularly,** removing weeds while they are still small. The hoe can be used between rows, but hand weeding will be necessary amongst plants.

**Water as necessary,** but don't waste water at the wrong times. Newly planted subjects (such as marrows etc.) may need water to settle them in after the root disturbance, but otherwise most fruit and vegetables do not need water unless they are actually flagging. The most productive time to water fruiting plants (including vegetables such as peas, beans, tomatoes, marrows etc.) is at flowering time as this aids fruit setting.

**Check for pests regularly.** Aphids are particularly troublesome, and blackfly can often be spotted on bean plants – around the flower stems on runner beans, and congregated in the shoot tips on broad beans. At the first sign of trouble on broad beans, pinch out the tips of the plants as long as they have set three or four clusters of pods; this will probably prevent further infestations. On runner beans, a strong jet of water directed at the colonies may be sufficient to remove them.

**Water runner beans thoroughly** while they are in full flower. The usual cause of flowers dropping off without setting pods is lack of water. It is not necessary to spray the flowers, as sometimes recommended – the soil is where the moisture is required.

**Continue planting out winter brassicas** as space becomes available. Water them in well.

**Earth up second early and maincrop potatoes** that were planted in spring, doing this job in several stages. The earliest-planted potates may soon be producing tubers of usable size. Do not lift any plants yet, but scrape away a little soil from around the largest plants and see how big the potatoes are.

**Stop cutting asparagus spears** now and allow the fern to develop, to build up the plants for next year. Continue removing all weeds in the asparagus bed.

**Some late crops can still be sown,** including French beans, Chinese cabbage, radishes, turnips, peas, spinach and quick-maturing carrots. Choose a partly shaded position, and keep the soil moist.

**Lettuce can also be sown now,** but the seed is affected by high temperature dormancy, which means that when soil and air temperatures reach a certain level, the seed will not germinate. Always choose a reasonably cool, moist, shady place for summer sowings of lettuce.

**Plant out pot-grown runner beans.** Start planting out celery and leeks.

**Aubergines, peppers and outdoor tomatoes** can be planted outdoors in sheltered positions.

**Spray fruit** against maggots. If you have previously had trouble with maggots in apples, codling moth is probably responsible. Spray the fruitlets now with derris, repeating the treatment in three weeks to catch any that were missed the first time round.

Containers filled with flowering plants can be used to brighten up many otherwise difficult areas. Regular watering is very important for all container-grown plants.

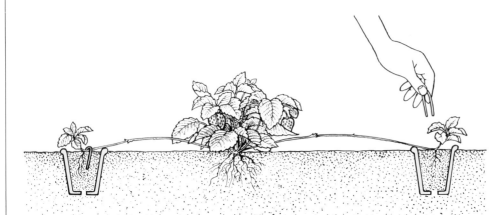

Strawberries are easily propagaged by pegging healthily runners into pots sunk into the soil around the main plant.

**Remove runners from strawberries** unless you want to propagate the plants. In that case, select the strongest runners and remove the rest (see above).

**Fruitlets of apples and pears** will thin themselves at this time of year, and you will find many fruitlets on the ground. If the fruit clusters still appear crowded after this natural drop, thin them out yourself, removing misshapen or small fruitlets to leave about three per spur.

**Summer prune bush fruit** such as redcurrants, whitecurrants and gooseberries – but not blackcurrants.

**In the greenhouse, ventilate freely.** The vents and door can probably remain fully open all day, even when the weather is cloudy.

**Damp down the paths and staging** regularly to provide humidity. Water greenhouse plants twice a day or more on sunny days.

**Feed tomatoes, cucumbers, melons etc.** as the fruits set. Feeding before this stage will just increase leafy growth.

**Whitefly** – small, white, moth-like insects – can be a real problem in greenhouses. If your greenhouse has been badly affected in the past, try a biological control. Supplies of a small parasitic wasp, *Encarsia formosa*, should be ordered as soon as the first whitefly are spotted.

If you prefer chemical control, pirimiphos methyl is the one to use. Repeated sprayings will be necessary.

**Sow *Primula malacoides*, calceolaria and cinerarias** for winter-flowering pot plants.

**Greenhouse cucumbers should not be pollinated,** or the fruits become misshapen and bitter. Remove all male flowers as soon as they are seen (see below). Train cucumbers by pinching out side shoots beyond two fruits, and pinching out further sideshoots (sub-laterals) at two pairs of leaves. Tie the shoots in to their supports.

Male flower                  Female flower

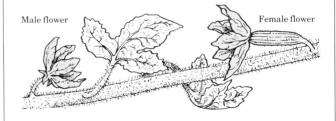

Remove male cucumber flowers as they form. Male and female flowers can be distinguished by the embryo fruit which forms behind the females.

# Mid-Summer

## FLOWERS AND ORNAMENTALS

**Deadhead flowering plants.** As well as making them look more attractive, removing dead flowers avoids the plant wasting energy in the unnecessary production of seeds. It will also help to prolong the flowering season; with most plants, the production of seeds signals that the purpose of flowering has been accomplished and there is no need to continue.

However, plants which produce attractive seedheads, hips, fruits or berries, should obviously not be deadheaded.

**Container-grown plants** can be planted successfully all the year round, but special care should be taken with those planted in summer. If the weather is very hot and dry they are probably better left in their pots until a colder, showery spell occurs.

Transplant with as little root disturbance as possible, but if root damage is unavoidable, trim back some of the top of the plant to balance out the roots and top growth. Water in very thoroughly, and keep the plant watered throughout the summer. Protect from drying winds.

**Continue to water lawns and border plants** if the weather is dry and there are no water restrictions. An occasional but thorough soaking is better than little and often when it comes to watering.

**Install garden lighting.** Warm, mid-summer evenings, filled with the fragrance of night-scented flowers, make it pleasant to be out of doors until late. Extend your time in the garden by installing garden lighting, to make eating and relaxing outside possible after dark.

For lighting areas inaccessible to the electricity supply, solar lights are available. These charge themselves on sunlight during daylight hours and give off a soft glow in the dark.

**The Madonna lily** *(Lilium candidum)* is one of the most beautiful and stately lilies. It is sometimes difficult to get established in the garden, and should be planted as early as possible. Look out for it in garden centres from mid-summer onwards, and buy and plant it immediately it is available. Unlike most bulbs, it should be planted shallowly, only just covering the nose with 3 cm (1 in) or so of soil.

**Semi-ripe cuttings** are a good way to propagate many flowering shrubs, and can be taken now. Suitable shoots are those that are still soft at the tip, but starting to ripen at their base; they should still be flexible. Take the cuttings early in the morning, dropping them straight into a polythene bag to prevent them drying out. Insert in sandy compost and keep moist and humid, covering the trays or pots with a plastic propagator top.

**Plants in hanging baskets** and other containers will still need very frequent watering and feeding. Baskets which are filled with roots may need to be taken down and dunked in a bucket of water to ensure that it penetrates the compost. Continue to liquid feed containers with a high-potash fertilizer such as rose or tomato feed.

**Disbud chrysanthemums and dahlias** for large, specimen blooms. The top bud on each stem should be retained, and the smaller buds in the leaf axils below should be nipped out with thumb and forefinger. This will produce a large, showy, single flower.

Some gardeners prefer the spray of smaller flowers that result from leaving the plants with

buds intact. Both types are good for cutting for the house and garden decoration.

**Continue to trim hedges** as necessary.

**Perennial and biennial flowers** that were sown in seedbeds in early summer should be thinned or pricked out to give them more space.

**If spring-flowering bulbs** need to be moved to make way for other plants, this is a safe time to lift them.

**Wisteria** is a magnificent flowering climber that all too often fails to perform well. The secret of getting it to flower reliably is summer pruning. On established plants that have filled the space allowed for them, sideshoots arising from the main stems should be reduced to about six leaves.

**Trim rock roses** (helianthemums) lightly with of shears, removing dead flowers and cutting back stems to encourage strong new growth.

**When cutting flowers for the house,** make sure the plants are well supplied with water beforehand. Make a clean cut across the stems – don't crush the stem bases – and stand the flowers in deep water up to their necks for several hours before arranging them. A pinch of sugar and a teaspoon of mild disinfectant in the water help the blooms to last.

## LAWNS

**Continue to cut lawns regularly** – twice a week if possible. When the grass is kept short like this, leave the grassbox off the mower and allow the clippings to lie on the surface.

◀ **Plant the beautiful Madonna lily,** *Lilium candidum*, as soon as bulbs appear in the shops. Unlike most bulbs, it requires shallow planting to do well.

▶ **There are few climbers more beautiful than a wisteria in full bloom.** Plants can be encouraged to flower well by pruning them in summer.

## FRUIT AND VEGETABLES

**Pick crops as they become available.** Peas, runner, broad and French beans, and courgettes, should all be picked regularly to keep them cropping well. If you are going on holiday, try to

# Making a fruit cage

Wild birds like fruit just as much as gardeners, and are not so fussy about waiting until it is ripe. To ensure that *you* harvest the majority of the crop, a fruit cage is an excellent idea.

If you grow a lot of fruit, a large, walk-in cage is ideal, though expensive. There are several manufacturers who will supply purpose-built cages. Supports are made from galvanized steel or aluminium tubing with joints to make linking the sections easy; there are also usually hinged doors for access to the cage. The package comes complete with netting, ground hooks, ties and so on, and is delivered ready for you to put together (see illustration). You can also make up your own cage from wooden posts and netting; this is a cheaper option but less convenient.

It is often worthwhile to make cages to protect small amounts of fruit – two or three currant bushes, or a row of raspberries, for example. Low strawberry cages are popular, as an entire crop of strawberries can be stolen by birds in no time.

The roof netting on walk-in cages should be removed or replaced with larger mesh netting in winter, as the weight of snow, if it falls, may break the netting and damage the supports.

arrange with a neighbour to pick them while you are away: if some fruits mature, production will slow down greatly.

**Lift potatoes, carrots, kohl rabi etc.** as soon as they are a usable size.

**Continue to plant leeks and winter greens** as the earliest crops finish and are cleared away.

**Thin seedlings as necessary.** Disturb carrots as little as possible while thinning, as the scent of the bruised foliage attracts adult carrot flies to lay their eggs.

**Continue to feed plants** as necessary.

**Train outdoor tomatoes,** tying them to their supports and sideshooting if necessary. Many outdoor varieties are grown as bushes that do not need sideshooting.

**Potato blight** can be a devastating disease. The first symptoms are dark spots or patches on the leaves, followed by yellowing of the foliage. It progresses amazingly quickly until the whole crop is a mass of yellow, wilted stems. Spores wash down into the soil and affect the tubers, which rot and will not keep.

Blight can be prevented by using a copper fungicide spray before any sign of the disease, but if it occurs when the potatoes are of usable size, the tops of the plants should be cut off and burned as soon as the first affected plant is seen. The whole crop can then be lifted without delay, before the spores are washed down to affect the tubers. Potato blight also affects outdoor tomatoes, producing rotten patches on the fruit.

**Globe artichokes** are a delicacy which also make statuesque and attractive border plants. Cut the heads with a short length of stem as soon as they are plump and rounded, but before the scales begin to open out.

**Make a last sowing** of quick-maturing carrots, sowing very thinly to avoid the need for thinning.

**Sow spring cabbage** in a seedbed.

# Making a wildlife garden

All gardens contain wildlife, whether we like it or not, but it is quite easy to make a garden more attractive to certain forms of wildlife that you want to encourage. Some creatures are useful in controlling plant pests; others are encouraged simply because we enjoy seeing them. Many gardeners also feel an obligation to help creatures whose natural habitats are under threat from our activities.

The wildlife garden should provide safety, shelter and food (see illustration). Safety means avoiding the use of potentially harmful chemicals; if not stopping altogether, at least being very selective about the products chosen. It also means not destroying established habitats – suddenly scything down a wild area, for example.

Shelter is very variable, depending on the type of creatures you wish to encourage. It may be nest boxes for small birds, rotting logs for a variety of insects and small mammals, or a box where a hedgehog can hibernate. Often it is simply an 'overgrown' area which remains undisturbed.

Food sources should mainly be growing plants; for example, berries for birds in winter, thistle seedheads for goldfinches, stinging nettles for the caterpillars of many butterflies. Butterflies themselves can be attracted to a range of nectar-producing plants such as buddleia and sedum; moths to night-scented plants like honeysuckle and tobacco.

Native wild plants and trees often support large populations of different creatures as well as being attractive in their own right. A compost heap is teeming with life, and produces a very valuable end product. Soil that is rich in organic matter harbours a varied and flourishing population of organisms.

One of the most valuable habitats is water, and a garden pond is a very worthwhile investment. Apart from the obvious creatures such as frogs, toads and newts, the water will be appreciated by birds who come to drink there, and by splendid insects such as dragonflies. Provide a shallow area for birds to drink and bathe. Keep the pond filled to the brim; a ramp will enable hedgehogs, who may occasionally fall into the water while drinking, to escape unharmed.

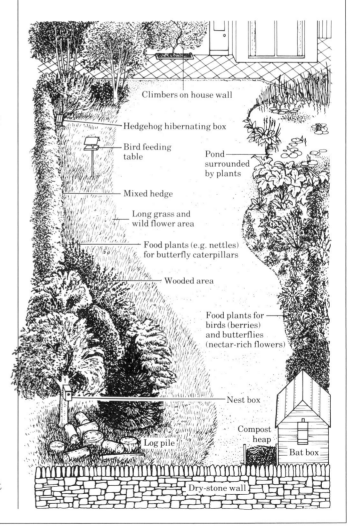

Climbers on house wall

Hedgehog hibernating box

Bird feeding table

Pond surrounded by plants

Mixed hedge

Long grass and wild flower area

Food plants (e.g. nettles) for butterfly caterpillars

Wooded area

Food plants for birds (berries) and butterflies (nectar-rich flowers)

Nest box

Compost heap

Log pile

Bat box

Dry-stone wall

**Continue to water runner beans,** giving the roots a good soaking to keep them cropping.

**Give apples a second derris spray** against codling moth.

**Begin earthing up** leeks and celery.

**Autumn-sown onions** will soon be ready for lifting. When the foliage starts to flop over, ease the plants up lightly with a fork to break the roots. Allow them to dry in the sun on the soil surface for a few days before storing them in wooden boxes in a well-ventilated place.

**Strawberry plants** begin to deteriorate after about three years, and the whole bed should be replaced by this time. The easiest way to do this is to raise new plants by layering, and replace a third of the bed each year.

Select healthy runners and peg the first plant-let on each runner into a pot of compost sunk into the soil by the parent plant. Cut off the runner beyond the plantlet. By the end of the summer these will have developed into sturdy young plants and can be separated from the parent.

**Strawberry plants not required for propagation** should have the foliage removed now, using shears or a nylon line trimmer. Be careful not to damage the crowns of the plants. Remove and burn the foliage; also the straw if it was used round the plants while they were fruiting.

**Silver leaf disease** attacks plums and related trees, and is difficult to control. The variety 'Victoria' is particularly susceptible to it. The symptoms are a subtle silvering of the foliage and a dark stain in the wood of affected branches.

Affected branches should be cut out during the summer months, while the sap is flowing. Cut back to where the branch is no longer stained. Do not prune plum trees in winter, as it is then that infection can take place.

◀ **Greenhouses need free ventilation and damping down as days become warmer.**

## GREENHOUSE AND HOUSE PLANTS

**Continue to water and feed** all plants as necessary.

**Ventilate the greenhouse freely,** and damp down the floor and staging regularly to keep the atmosphere humid. Check that shading is still doing its job.

**Continue to check plants for pests,** taking action as soon as any are found.

**Prick out seedlings** from earlier sowings as necessary. Wait until the seedlings can be hand-led easily, but don't allow them to become over-crowded in the trays. Shade newly pricked out plants with sheets of newspaper for a few days.

**Pot up pelargonium cuttings** once they are well rooted.

**Sow herbs** like basil, marjoram, thyme and parsley to grow in pots indoors for the winter months.

**Some tender plants enjoy a spell outside** in a sheltered place in mid-summer. This helps to ripen the wood of plants such as jasmine, ensuring good winter flowering.

**Blossom end rot** is a disorder of tomatoes (and to a lesser extent peppers) which causes a hard, shrivelled, black area at the base of the fruit, where the flower was. It is usually caused by the lack of water at flowering time.

Plants in growing bags are most often affected because the small amount of compost does not hold a large reserve of water. If you are out at work all day and unable to water plants regularly, it would be better to grow tomatoes in the greenhouse border or in larger pots of compost.

**Remove faded leaves** from the base of tomatoes.

**Fan heaters** can be useful in summer if the fan will run without heating. The fans keep the air moving, helping to keep down temperatures and, more importantly, prevent fungus diseases which love still, moist air.

# Late Summer

## FLOWERS AND ORNAMENTALS

**Continue to disbud chrysanthemums** for large, single blooms.

**Trim evergreen hedges** for the last time before autumn. Late trimming will result in soft young growth which will be prone to damage by autumn and winter frosts.

**Take cuttings** from plants in containers outside, such as fuchsias, pelargoniums, helichrysum. These usually root quickly at this time, and will provide good plants for overwintering in a frost-free greenhouse or in a light position in the home.

**Continue feeding and watering** plants in containers regularly to prolong flowering and keep the colour going until the frosts put an end to the display.

**Order spring-flowering bulbs** from catalogues if you have not already done so. Don't forget to order bulbs for flowering in pots and bowls in the home during the winter.

**Continue deadheading** border plants and tie stems in to their supports. Cut back any ungainly, straggly growths. Plants in tubs and hanging baskets should also be deadheaded and pruned back where necessary.

## FRUIT AND VEGETABLES

**Thin seedlings** as necessary. Do not allow plants to become too crowded in the rows.

**Continue watering crops** as necessary, giving a thorough soaking with the hose. In dry conditions, water the drills before sowing seeds.

**Continue harvesting vegetables** such as beetroot, potatoes, carrots, courgettes, peas, runner beans, French beans, marrows and so on. Do not leave crops to go past their best and probably reduce further cropping.

**Store gluts of fruit and vegetables** by freezing, drying or bottling, or by making jams, pickles and chutneys.

**Stop outdoor tomatoes** by pinching out the growing tips. Tomatoes produced now will not have sufficient time to ripen, and stopping will divert the plant's energy into ripening those already on the plant.

**Continue to feed tomatoes,** both outdoors and in the greenhouse, with a high-potash liquid fertilizer every seven to ten days.

**Blanch leeks** to give a good length of tender white stem by drawing soil carefully up around them as they grow. Take care not to get soil down the centres of the plants, or they will be very gritty to eat.

**Ripen onions** from early sowings by bending over the leaves at the neck of the bulbs. It is a good idea to wait until the leaves on the first bulb fall over naturally, as then you will be sure the plants are ready.

After two or three weeks the onions will be ready to lift and store. Prise them out of the soil with a fork and leave them on the soil surface for a few days to dry (as long as the weather allows). Once dry, rub off any soil clinging to them and tie them in ropes by twisting the old foliage together, or spread them out in trays or boxes. Keep them cool but frost free.

**Sow spinach** for a spring crop. At this time of year, the sowing must be of a prickly-seeded variety, as this withstands hot, dry conditions better than normal spinach. Even so, on free-draining soils, summer-sown spinach may run to seed almost as soon as it has germinated. In these conditions, try growing spinach beet instead. This is not true spinach but a variety of beetroot; the leaves are rather coarser and not so tender as spinach but it makes a very acceptable substitute when cooked in the same way. Like beetroot, two or three seeds should be sown at each station and the seedlings later thinned to the strongest.

**Sow more spring cabbage** to follow on from the mid-summer sowing. These can be planted out as space is cleared in the vegetable plot.

**Sow Japanese onions.** These varieties over-winter well to give the earliest crops next year. They are not always successful, but they are well worth trying in a sheltered place.

**Pick apples** as they ripen. Early varieties do not keep for long and should be eaten as soon as they will part readily from the tree; to check ripeness, lift the fruit gently to see whether it comes away easily at the spur.

**Plant strawberries.** This is the best time to plant strawberries if you want a good crop next summer. Plants can be obtained as cold-stored runners or rooted runners in small pots; both should establish satisfactorily if the soil is well prepared, with plenty of well-rotted compost dug in beforehand. Buy certified plants to ensure that the stock is healthy and free from virus to start with – though once planted it can soon be infected with virus diseases, which are transmitted by aphids.

Plants can be grown single spaced or in matted rows. Matted rows give a higher overall yield, but the individual berries are smaller. Plant single spaced plants at 30–38 cm (12–15 in) and remove runners that are not required for propagation as they appear. For matted rows, plant at 38–45 cm (15–18 in) and train the runners into the rows, allowing them to root. Plant strawberries very firmly, and water them sufficiently to enable them to get established quickly.

# Summer pruning

Summer pruning is mainly carried out on fruit trees which need to have their growth restricted – forms such as cordons and espaliers. If they are not pruned in summer, the trees soon become a mass of unproductive shoots.

Start summer pruning in mid-summer, when the bases of the shoots are just starting to become woody. Laterals (side shoots) are cut back to four leaves above the basal cluster of leaves (a). Shoots which have been pruned in previous years are cut back to one leaf above the basal cluster (b). The cuts should be made cleanly just above a leaf, and the leaves themselves should not be damaged.

This pruning encourages the formation of fruiting spurs. As the trees age, some of the established spurs become crowded and less fruitful. When this happens they can be removed, as new spur systems should be constantly being formed to replace them.

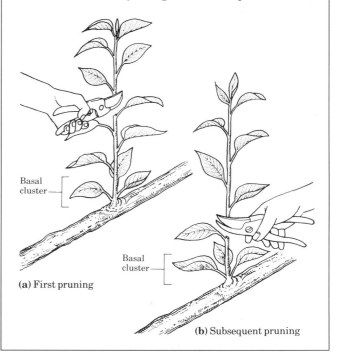

Basal cluster

**(a)** First pruning

Basal cluster

**(b)** Subsequent pruning

**Prune summer-fruiting raspberries,** cutting back all the canes that have carried fruit to ground level. New canes should be trained in to the wire supports to provide fruit for the following year. Any canes that are growing in the pathway, too far away to train in, should be cut out. Thin out the young shoots if they are very crowded, keeping the strongest ones.

## GREENHOUSE AND HOUSE PLANTS

**Sow cyclamen seed.** Soak the seed overnight before sowing, then rinse it in running water for 10 minutes; this helps improve germination rates.

**Start resting cyclamen tubers** into growth. Remove old foliage, repot tubers, water the plants, and mist the tops of the tubers with a very fine spray of clear water.

**Pot up freesia corms** for scented winter flowers as soon as they are available.

**Pick melons** as they ripen. When ripe, the fruit begins to crack around the stalk end, but a quick sniff at the fruits is the best guide as to when they are ready for picking. Ripe melons have an unmistakeable, rich, heady scent.

**Clear out cucumber plants** as soon as all the fruits have been picked. Tomatoes, peppers, aubergines etc. should be removed as soon as the crop is over.

**Watch out for cooler nights** as we move towards autumn: grey mould disease thrives in moist, cool, still air. Remove dead and dying plant material promptly, and keep the greenhouse well ventilated.

**Sow schizanthus** to provide winter-flowering pot plants. Keep the seedlings in a cool, airy place.

◀ Ripe melons, fresh-picked from the greenhouse, are a real treat. An unmistakable, heady scent will tell you when they are ready for harvest.

▶ Autumn has its own particular beauty, with fiery crimson and gold shades as well as the more subtle russets and browns of dying foliage.

# · 3 ·
# Autumn

Sometimes summer slips into autumn almost imperceptibly. The weather may be warm and sunny, often more pleasant and settled than it has been in past weeks. Flower borders are still vibrant with colour; butterflies flit drunkenly about the fallen apples. But there is a crispness to the early morning air; nights come early and are cool. The tell-tale autumn flowers give the brightest colour in the garden, and blackberries glisten dark and ripe in the scrambled hedgerows.

There is a flurry of activity from birds and animals. It is the silly season for squirrels; all summer they have remained stealthily in the trees, out of sight, but now they caper across lawns and scurry through the plants without caring who sees them, bent upon some urgent message from their internal clocks. Birds, too, begin feeding with an earnestness upon fruits and berries, intent upon stocking up for the lean season ahead.

Dew lies heavy and silver on the grass in the morning, and fungi appear as if by magic, overnight. Puffballs swell, solid, round and fat: fairy rings push up their fragile caps on delicate, translucent stems. Other fungi are busy among the summer's debris of fruits and flowers and foliage, stealthily infiltrating the tissues, breaking them down to a dank, damp, rotting mass, helped by an army of insects and other tiny creatures.

The large, purple and pink flowers of colchicums are too heavy for their delicate stems, and frequently they topple over when in their prime. Hardy cyclamen have no such problem; their cheerful flowers last for many weeks. But soon their pastel colours are eclipsed by the foliage of deciduous trees as the leaves begin their slow process of dying. The first nip of frost signals the beginning of the best of the display. Scarlet, yellow, flame, purple, crimson: in a good year, autumn colours can be breathtaking. Around the time of the equinox, though, mellow autumn days often disappear to give us a foretaste of winter, with gales stripping the trees bare in an abrupt and violent end to their performance.

It's time for gardeners to start preparing for the winter, too. The autumn clear-up should provide plenty of material for the compost heap, but there is something ritualistic about an autumn bonfire that keeps people lighting up. Few things are more evocative of autumn than the tang of bonfire smoke drifting on the crisp, clear air.

It's time to harvest the last of the season's crops: to clear away the spent plants, expose the bare earth once more. Whatever the successes and failures of the past season, it will soon be time to start again. In the ever-shortening days, the gardener working on his plot is not clearing up after the summer – he's really getting ready for the spring.

# A new lawn from turf

Using turf to make a new lawn gives you instant results – although the new lawn should be treated carefully until it gets established. Autumn is the best time to carry this out, but it is also possible to turf in spring.

Soil preparation is as important as for a lawn from seed. Dig the whole site over thoroughly, removing all perennial weeds and weed roots. Incorporate some long-lasting fertilizer such as bonemeal, and rake the site level, breaking down clods with the back of the rake. Water to thoroughly moisten the soil a few days before you intend laying the turf. Get all the preparation done in advance, so that when the turf arrives, it can be laid as soon as possible – it can remain stacked for a day or two at most. Try to ensure the turves are delivered close to the new lawn area, to minimize the amount of carrying required.

Start laying the lawn at the end nearest the turf stack. Unroll or unfold each turf and lay it on the soil, firming it with a few light blows from a turf beetle (a flat piece of wood on a stick) or a rake held

upright. Butt each turf up to the next so there is no gap; the turves will shrink slightly after laying anyway. Overlap the proposed edges of the lawn on all sides. Always lay the turves straight; any curves required will be cut with an edging iron later.

When you finish each row, lay the next so that the joints are staggered – bonding the turves like a brick wall. Remember to butt the long sides of each row up to the previous row of turves. Use a plank to walk over the newly laid turves as you work your way to the other end of the lawn (a). Cut the turves as necessary with a sharp edging iron. Sometimes a small piece of turf will need to be cut to fill the row. This piece should never be put at the edge of the lawn but should be set further in the row so that the edge turf is at least half size.

Once the whole area has been covered, brush in a topdressing of a loam, sand and peat mixture, working it into the joints between the turves (b). Water the new lawn well, and continue watering regularly until it is established. After a day or two, use a sharp edging iron to cut round the edges of the lawn.

**(a)**

**(b)**

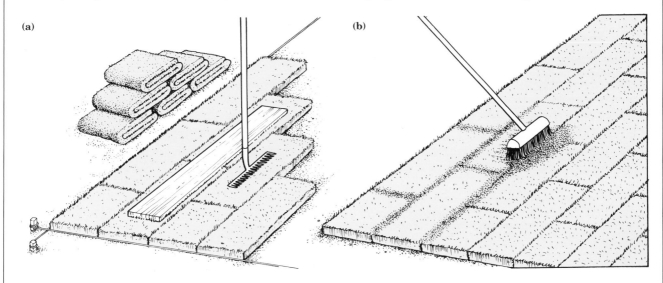

# Early Autumn

## FLOWERS AND ORNAMENTALS

**Late-flowering perennials** help to extend the summer just a little longer, bringing a last burst of colour to the border before the autumn leaf tints of trees and shrubs take over. Michaelmas daisies come into their own, with some rich pinks as well as the more familiar blues and purples: watch out for mildew, which often spoils the foliage of these plants. A fungicide spray at the very first sign of powdery white patches should hold the disease in check.

The broad, flat, yellow heads of achillea ('Gold Plate' is the best-known variety) are long lasting both in the border and when cut. The fiery orange tones of crocosmia complement yellow and orange daisy-like heleniums and rudbeckias, and chrysanthemums and dahlias stand out well, with their wide range of colours – gold, orange, bronze, red, yellow, pink, white.

**Colour from bulbs** is more often associated with spring, but several make their appearance now. The delicate pink, white and purple flowers of hardy cyclamen can carpet a semi-shaded spot under trees or shrubs, while the fragile, delicate flowers of colchicum (autumn crocus) are usually a little later to appear. There are also some true crocuses that flower in autumn; these begin to appear from mid-autumn onwards.

*Nerine bowdenii* carries rounded heads of startling pink, trumpet-shaded blooms on tall stems

◀ The lovely pink trumpets of *Nerine bowdenii* need a sheltered position to produce the best display. The base of a south-facing wall is an ideal place to plant the bulbs.

and does well against a sheltered wall. *Amaryllis belladonna* has larger flowers, carried around the same time, and appreciates a sheltered spot even more.

**Prepare the ground** for planting trees and shrubs in the dormant season. Dig the soil over thoroughly and deeply, breaking up any hard 'pan' that may impede drainage. Remove all weed roots you may come across, and dig in plenty of organic matter such as rotted garden compost or manure.

**Sow grass seed** to make a new lawn or to restore worn patches on an existing one. Spike a bare patch thoroughly with a garden fork, then scratch up the surface slightly before sowing the seed. Mixing the seed with slightly moistened peat helps ensure even, rapid germination; spread the mix over the prepared area and if necessary protect it from birds with cotton threaded over short canes.

It is important to try to obtain the right type of grass seed for patching a lawn; a different seed mix can give a very noticeable patch of a different colour and leaf texture to the rest of the lawn. On high quality ornamental lawns it is best to do any patching required with turf, where it is easier to select a good match.

When sowing a new lawn, always keep a note of the seed mix (the different types of grass and their proportions will be listed on the pack) and the supplier, in case you need to do any repair work in the future.

**Rose hips** can be as valuable as the flowers through the autumn months, and there is a wide range of different shapes and sizes. *Rosa rugosa* is often grown as a hedge; it has vigorous, sturdy stems with robust, crinkly textured foliage. The loosely formed, scented flowers are followed by large, round, fat hips that look like bunches of tomatoes nestling among the clear yellow of the

53

autumn leaves. *Rosa moyesii* has elongated, flask-shaped hips which are particularly showy, set off by reddish stems and deep green leaves. The apple rose, *R. pomifera*, also known as *R. villosa*, has smaller, dark red, peculiarly bristly fruits that last well.

Many other rose varieties, but particularly the species roses, have attractive fruits. If you want to enjoy the hips, remember not to deadhead the plants as the flowers fade!

**Pinks (dianthus) layered earlier** can be lifted and transplanted when they are well rooted.

**Plant spring-flowering bulbs.** As soon as summer starts to reach its end, garden centres become filled with bulbs in many varieties. The earlier you buy them, the better the selection will be, and the better quality the bulbs will be, too. They soon deteriorate in the warm conditions, and bulbs in 'self-select' bins can be bruised and damaged as customers sort through them. Bulbs that arrive by mail order should also be planted as soon as they arrive. Remember that it is not natural for bulbs to be out of the soil for any period of time.

It is important to plant bulbs at the right depth for good flowering. After a dry summer, the ground is often hard, making deep planting tough going. Persevere; water the ground thoroughly beforehand if necessary. Special planting tools are available to make the job easier. Make sure you buy one that is well made and sturdy, as cheap tools can bend and break at the first hint of hard work.

For naturalizing bulbs in turf, a long-handled bulb planter is invaluable. These are expensive and only available from specialist suppliers (some bulb firms sell them) but they are well worth the money if you have a large area to plant up.

**Take cuttings of evergreens.** Choose ripened shoots about 15 cm (6 in) long and pull them away from the branch with a small heel of bark. Dip them in rooting powder and insert them in a box of sandy compost, 5 cm (2 in) deep, and firm them in well. Put the box in a cold frame, unheated greenhouse or sheltered spot in the garden.

**Sow hardy annuals** in sheltered positions where they are to flower next year. These showings will give very early flowers.

**Fungi on lawns** start to appear as the days cool. These mainly live on decaying matter below the surface of the turf, and while some can be unsightly, they are not usually of any significance. They have a short season, and can be swept away if necessary. Fairy rings are more serious, as deep green, very noticeable rings of turf develop where they grow. Control is very difficult, and an application of fertilizer to green up the rest of the grass and disguise the rings is often the best way to deal with them.

**Berries on plants** are attractive to children as well as gardeners. Several are poisonous, and though few cause serious illness, they can result

| · BULB PLANTING DEPTHS · | | |
|---|---|---|
| **Bulb** | **Planting depth** | **Spacing** |
| Alliums | 10 cm (4 in) | 20 cm (8 in) |
| *Anemone blanda* | 5 cm (2 in) | 10 cm (4 in) |
| Chionodoxa | 8 cm (3 in) | 10 cm (4 in) |
| Crocus | 8 cm (3 in) | 10 cm (4 in) |
| Eranthis | 5 cm (2 in) | 10 cm (4 in) |
| Erythronium | 10 cm (4 in) | 10 cm (4 in) |
| *Fritillaria imperialis* | 20cm (8 in) | 30 cm (12 in) |
| *F. meleagris* | 10 cm (4 in) | 15 cm (6 in) |
| Galanthus | 8 cm (3 in) | 8 cm (3 in) |
| Hyacinth | 15 cm (6 in) | 20 cm (8 in) |
| Iris (Dutch, Spanish, English) | 15 cm (6 in) | 15 cm (6 in) |
| Lilium | 23 cm (9 in) | 30 cm (12 in) |
| Muscari | 8 cm (3 in) | 10 cm (4 in) |
| Narcissus | 15 cm (6 in) | 20 cm (8 in) |
| Scilla | 10 cm (4 in) | 10 cm (4 in) |
| Tulip | 15 cm (6 in) | 20 cm (8 in) |

in unpleasant stomach upsets if eaten. Some are potentially fatal. Berried plants to beware of include yew, daphne, honeysuckle, privet, arum and the nightshades.

## FRUIT AND VEGETABLES

**Plant spring cabbages.** Continue planting these out as space becomes available, and make sure they are very well firmed in to the soil.

**Continue picking runner beans.** These should crop until the first frosts as long as they have been picked regularly throughout the summer.

**Marrow and pumpkins** can be cut for storing before the frosts arrive. Make sure they are not damaged, and store in a cool, dry, dark, airy place. As long as they are ripe, they will keep quite well.

**Earth up celery and leeks.** Continue with this job as necessary to give a good length of blanched stem.

**Lift maincrop potatoes.** Potatoes can be lifted for storing on a dry day. Dig them up with a fork, setting aside any damaged ones to use up straight away. Allow the tubers to dry on the soil surface for a very short time, then brush off excess soil and store them in paper sacks in a frost-free shed. Make sure you lift all the tubers or you will have a lot of unwanted 'volunteers' growing through your crops next year.

**Carrots and beetroot** can also be lifted for storing, if required, about this time, too. Twist off the top growth and store the roots in boxes of sand or dry peat to keep them plump.

**Thin out any late-sown seedlings** of spinach and lettuce as it becomes necessary.

**Pick all the fruit from outdoor tomatoes** before the frosts. Unripe fruit may ripen indoors if it has started to change colour to a pale greenish yellow. Space the tomatoes well apart on

# Making compost

Composting is the aerobic decomposition of organic matter. Virtually everything organic will rot down eventually, but some substances are not suitable for the compost heap. Avoid woody prunings, which would take too long to rot (unless they are shredded mechanically): also avoid diseased plants, perennial weed roots and seeding annual weeds. In theory, temperatures within the compost heap are high enough to kill all these, but unless a heap is very carefully made, this is not always the case.

A compost bin helps to keep the heap tidy. It can be a simple structure such as three sides of chicken wire on sturdy posts, or a more elaborate construction of wooden slats. Make it as large as possible, and ideally ensure that the structure allows some air to the heap while helping to retain warmth. Two bins, side by side, are best.

Build the heap of garden refuse such as soft prunings, vegetable peelings and crop remains. Lawn mowings can be added, but mix them thoroughly with more bulky waste, otherwise they pack together too tightly for proper decomposition. Add a layer of garden soil every 20 cm (8 in) or so. Continue like this until the bin is full, then top off with garden soil and start the next bin.

The compost is ready to use when it is dark and crumbly with no unpleasant smell and no identifiable plant remains – usually the following autumn.

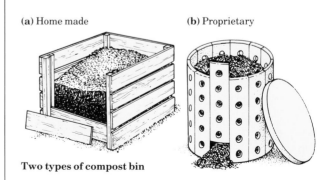

**(a)** Home made   **(b)** Proprietary

**Two types of compost bin**

a tray and keep them in a fairly cool place, checking them over frequently to remove any that are rotting. They may continue to ripen slowly for two months or so. Fruits that are still quite green are best made into chutney.

**Pick apples and pears** over the next few weeks. If the fruit is to store well it must not be damaged in any way. Pick by cradling each fruit in the palm and lifting it; if it is ripe, it will separate easily from the tree. Place it in a box or basket lined with a cloth to avoid bruising.

Apples can be stored in single layers in stacked trays, or in strong cardboard boxes with layers separated by a thick wadding of newspaper. Each fruit can be individually wrapped in paper or just well spaced so that none of the fruits touch. Apples also store well in plastic bags. Tie the bags at the top and make half a dozen holes in the plastic with a pencil. Store in a cool, dark shed or room.

Pears need more careful storing than apples. They must be handled even more gently, and placed in single layers only. Inspect them regularly and remove those that are starting to ripen straight away – they must be eaten within a day or two or they will go soft and 'sleepy'.

**Wasps** can be a problem on ripe fruits and you should inspect fallen fruits carefully before eating them. Wasps can be trapped in sticky jam jars, half filled with water and hung in the branches of

◀ Apples will store well if they are individually wrapped in paper and placed in strong cardboard boxes in a cool but frost-free place. Only perfectly sound fruits should be stored.

▶ An ideal informal hedge for a seaside garden, *Fuchsia magellanica* has a long flowering season.

# Planting a hedge

Hedges may be planted for several reasons:
- to mark a boundary
- to provide privacy
- to deter intruders
- to provide shelter
- for their decorative value.

Any hedge is going to be a long-lived feature, so preparation of the soil must be thorough. Using a line to keep the edges straight, take out a trench and fork over the base (a). Add as much well-rotted manure or compost as you have available, plus a sprinkling of a slow-acting fertilizer such as bonemeal.

Set the hedging plants in the trench at the correct depth (they should be planted to the nursery soil mark which should be visible on the stem). If necessary, provide them with temporary canes for support (b). Return the soil to the trench, shaking the first few spadefuls of soil down between the roots of the plants. Tread the soil down as you gradually fill in the trench (c). In exposed positions, provide some form of temporary windbreak while the plants become established, especially for evergreens.

Buy plants that are about 30–90 cm (1–3 ft) tall, depending on variety. Very small plants are cheaper, but take longer to produce a useful hedge. Large plants do not establish so quickly, and after a few seasons, smaller plants will have caught them up for a cheaper outlay.

There are many plants suitable for hedging, depending on the size and type of hedge you require. These are just a few suggestions.

### Formal hedges
Privet (*Ligustrum ovalifolium*)
Holly (*Ilex aquifolium*)
Shrubby honeysuckle (*Lonicera nitida*)

### Informal hedges
Rose (*Rosa rugosa* and many other varieties)
Barberry (*Berberis stenophylla*)
Rosemary (*Rosmarinus officinalis*)

### Dwarf hedges
Lavender (*Lavandula officinalis*)
Box (*Buxus sempervirens*)
Cotoneaster (*Cotoneaster microphyllus*)

### Hedges for seaside gardens
Escallonia (*Escallonia macrantha*)
Fuchsia (*Fuchsia magellanica*)
Sea buckthorn (*Hippophae rhamnoides*)

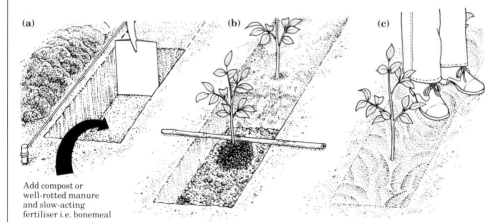

**(a)** Add compost or well-rotted manure and slow-acting fertiliser i.e. bonemeal

**(b)**

**(c)**

A hedge is a long-lasting garden feature, so the ground needs to be thoroughly prepared before planting. Always set plants at the same level they were grown in the nursery; you should be able to see the soil mark on the stem.

fruit trees, but it is doubtful whether this actually helps to reduce the numbers or just attracts more.

**Butterflies** also like fallen apples, and are usually more welcome than wasps. Red admirals, particularly, can be seen in great numbers around fruit trees in early autumn, whereas small tortoiseshells, peacocks and others are more likely to be attracted to the pink heads of late-flowering *Sedum spectabile* in the flower borders.

**Strawberries** can still be planted for a good crop next year, but it pays to get them in as soon as possible now.

## GREENHOUSE AND HOUSE PLANTS

**Check greenhouse temperatures** at night with a maximum/minimum thermometer to see when heating is necessary. Give heating systems a final check over to ensure they are in working order. Thermostatically controlled systems can be switched on to avoid being caught out by an early frost.

**Greenhouse vents** will still need to be open on most days in sunny weather, but should be closed in the early evening.

**Tender plants** which have spent the summer outside should be moved back to the greenhouse, conservatory or home before the first frosts. Remove dead and dying foliage and check the plants for pests before moving them back inside.

**Plants bulbs for forcing** for the home and keep them in a cold, dark place until the shoots are showing through the compost. Plant bulbs for a long-lasting show of colour through winter.

**Pot up cyclamen seedlings** that were sown earlier into individual pots.

**Sow a range of annuals** to grow in pots for winter colour. The seedlings will need a position in good light.

# Feeding plants

Plants manufacture food for energy from sunlight, but for this manufacturing process to work, minerals from the soil are also needed. Most soils contain sufficient quantities of minerals to keep the plants growing, but sometimes we need to supplement them.

The major plant nutrients are nitrogen, phosphorus and potassium (often abbreviated to NPK). Nitrogen is important for leafy growth: phosphorus for root development, among other essential processes, and potassium is involved in flowering and fruiting. Other minerals needed in fairly large quantities are calcium (lime) and magnesium. Minerals needed in tiny quantities are known as trace elements (micro-nutrients), and include iron, manganese, boron and molybdenum. Each of these has a vital role to play in the functioning of the plant.

Nutrient deficiencies can be identified by the plant failing to thrive in some way: major symptoms are shown below.

| Nutrient | Deficiency symptom |
| --- | --- |
| Nitrogen | Small, pale green or yellow foliage, sometimes purplish-blue or tinged with red. |
| Phosphorus | Small leaves, sometimes spotted with an overall bronzing, falling early. |
| Potassium | Failure to flower; fruits small and sparsely produced; browning of leaf edges. |
| Calcium | Most common on tomatoes, where it leads to blossom end rot on the fruits. |
| Magnesium | Yellowing between the veins of the older leaves, which fall early. |
| Iron | Marked yellowing between the leaf veins; common on chalky soils. |

# Mid-Autumn

## FLOWERS AND ORNAMENTALS

**Autumn colour from foliage** now starts to come into its own. Its season is brief, but spectacular. Acers are among the most notable trees and shrubs, particularly the rich crimson *Acer japonicum*, with lobed leaves of varying shapes according to variety. *Acer griseum* is also spectacular in autumn, and its shaggy bark is a pleasure throughout the winter and the rest of the year, too. The staghorn sumach, *Rhus typhina*; is among the most brilliant of autumn shrubs, so that it can almost be forgiven for assuming the appearance of an ungainly hat-stand for the rest of the year, though its habit of throwing up a thicket of suckers is less easy to overlook.

*Parrotia persica*, liquidamber and *Nyssa sylvatica* are all grown specifically for their autumn foliage and make pleasant, though not particularly significant, trees for the rest of the year. Witch hazels have the bonus of strongly scented winter flowers as well as the clear yellow autumn leaves, and trees of the *Prunus* family may have flowers and fruits as well as good autumn colour. When it comes to climbers, Virginia creeper and its relative Boston ivy are outstanding. If you have a warm, sheltered wall, try the Chinese Virginia creeper, *Parthenocissus henryana*; the leaf veins are picked out attractively in creamy pink.

**Autumn leaves** become fallen leaves, and in some years an ill-timed storm can put paid to autumn colour very quickly. Fallen leaves must be removed from lawns, where they will smother the grass, and paths and steps, where they can become dangerously slippery. They are easier to deal with while they are dry and crisp than when they are rain-sodden and slimy. They can be composted to make leafmould, but take longer to rot down than much other garden refuse.

**Tidy border plants.** Remove dead flowerheads and foliage and weed between the plants. Put the rubbish on the compost heap rather than burning it. For large beds and borders this task can be undertaken gradually over the autumn.

**Clear away summer bedding plants** and replace them with spring bedding. The most popular plants are wallflowers, primulas and polyanthus, and forget-me-nots, often underplanted with tulips. Before planting, clear away all weeds, fork the bed over and add some garden compost if available, and a sprinkling of long-lasting fertilizer, such as bonemeal.

**Bare-root trees and shrubs** are those lifted from open ground – in other words, not grown in containers. They can only be planted in the dormant season, but they are generally cheaper than container-grown plants, and larger specimens can be obtained. They can be planted from mid or late autumn right through until spring, avoiding only freezing spells and times when the soil is waterlogged.

The roots should not be allowed to dry out, and should be covered with sacking or plastic while they are out of the ground. If the soil is not suitable for planting straight away, bare-root plants should be 'heeled in' to a spare piece of ground while they are waiting. This means digging a shallow hole and just covering the roots with soil.

▶ *Nyssa sylvatica*, **sometimes known as the tupelo, comes into its own in autumn, with its striking, richly coloured foliage.**

# Making a vegetable garden

A few vegetables can be fitted in to almost any size garden, growing in a border amongst the flowers. However, a vegetable plot will enable you to grow a much wider range.

Site the vegetable plot in an open, sunny position. Make it as large as practical (bearing in mind that the whole area is likely to have to be dug over every year). If an area of lawn is to be sacrificed, strip off the turf neatly (it can be used elsewhere) and double dig or rotavate the soil beneath (see illustration). If a border or previously unused piece of ground is being converted, remove top growth and then cultivate deeply, making sure you remove all weed roots. Add as much well-rotted garden compost or manure as there is available.

Leave the soil roughly dug over winter, then in early spring rake it down level ready for sowing. Rake in an application of general purpose fertilizer. As digging always brings plenty of weed seeds to the surface where they can germinate, there will soon be a flush of weed seedlings; wait until these have germinated, then hoe or spray them off with herbicide. You are now ready to make your first sowings.

**When stripping turf to make a vegetable garden, mark out the area with pegs and string. Using a sharp edging iron and taut string as a guide (a), cut the grass into strips about 30 cm × 1 m (1 ft × 3¼ ft), then use a spade to undercut each turf and expose the soil underneath. When all the grass has been lifted, double dig the soil or use a cultivator (b).**

(a)

(b)

**Long-lasting fertilizers** are best for use in autumn. They are normally applied to the base of planting holes so they are near the roots of new plants; instead of releasing all their nutrients straight away, they gradually release them over a long period. Bonemeal is one of the most popular, supplying phosphates. There are also several proprietary planting fertilizers and slow release formulations which rely on temperature and moisture to gradually break down the granules. Read the back of the packs carefully to find those that are suitable for autumn use.

**Berries** help provide colour and interest throughout the autumn and sometimes into the winter as well. It is always disappointing when berries fail to form, and the plants remain resolutely and boringly green. There may be several reasons for non-berrying.

Some plants, such as holly, have male and female forms; male forms do not carry berries but may be necessary for fertilization and subsequent fruiting of females. A lone, berryless holly bush may be a male, or a female in need of a partner. There are named male and female varieties, though as someone with a strange sense of humour has named male hollies 'Golden Queen' and 'Silver Queen' and a female 'Golden King', it is not surprising there are so many berryless bushes about!

Skimmias also need male and female plants to produce berries, and a group of one male to three females is recommended. A good male variety is *S. japonica* 'Rubella', which throughout the winter carries panicles of decorative red buds opening to white flowers in spring.

Another reason for failure to berry is failure to flower. As flowers of berrying plants are often insignificant, this can easily be overlooked. An early spring application of sulphate of potash can work wonders on shy flowering plants, but a move to a more open, sunny position may sometimes be necessary.

**Tulips and hyacinths** are planted later than the other spring-flowering bulbs such as narcissi, and now is the time to do it. Try some of the very colourful, short-stemmed 'botanical' tulips as well as the more popular tall varieties. Some, such as varieties of *Tulipa griegii*, have very attractive, veined foliage.

**Protect newly planted and tender shrubs** from strong winds. Evergreens are particularly vulnerable, as winds whip moisture away from the leaf surface, leading to ugly scorching and sometimes to the death of the plants. Hessian or plastic sacking, set up on sturdy poles, can do a lot to protect plants in exposed positions.

**Take hardwood cuttings.** These cuttings are taken from fully ripened wood of the current year's growth, from 15–30 cm (6–12 in) long. Remove faded foliage and insert the cuttings in a trench in a sheltered part of the garden, pushing them 8–10 cm (3–4 in) deep. Firm them in well and leave them *in situ* until the following autumn. Soft fruits, especially currants and gooseberries, are easily propagated by this method.

LAWNS

**Continue laying turf** to make new lawns. This can be done whenever the weather is not frosty. Worn patches on established lawns can also be replaced with new turves now: cut out a straight-sided section round the damaged area and carefully remove it to the correct depth. Rake over the soil underneath, building it up to the right level if necessary, and place the new turf, cut to exactly the right size, on top. Firm it down well.

**Repair worn lawn edges.** Where edges have been damaged or have crumbled away, cut a rectangular section around the damaged area with an edging iron. Carefully lift the rectangle, turn it round so that the damaged piece is facing inwards, and replace it so that the straight edge lines up with the edge of the lawn. Re-sow the damaged part with lawn seed if it is large.

FRUIT AND VEGETABLES

**Continue gathering fruit crops** as they are ready.

**Stake Brussels sprouts** and other tall brassicas such as kale in exposed positions.

**Cover French beans** with cloches to extend the cropping season if the plants are still in good condition.

**Take hardwood cuttings** of gooseberries and currants.

**Finish earthing up** leeks and celery if the final earthing up has not already been done.

**Remove weeds** from the fruit and vegetable plots, particularly perennial weeds, which should have the roots dug out. Once the tops die down for winter it is impossible to see where the weeds are, and you will have to rely on finding the roots during winter digging.

**Cut down asparagus fern** once it has turned yellow. Weed the asparagus bed thoroughly before winter. Because asparagus is a perennial crop, weeds can be a problem unless you keep on top of them throughout the year – there is no chance to dig the bed over to turf weeds out, and few weedkillers are suitable for using on the bed.

**Leave some turnips in the ground** to provide turnip tops in spring. These make a tasty green vegetable early in the year.

**Mark rows of parsnips** to help you locate them once the tops have died off. Parsnips can be left in the ground throughout the winter, though some can be dug up for storing for those times the ground is frozen solid and you are unable to lift the roots.

**Apply lime** to vacant parts of the vegetable plot unless your soil is chalky. Liming does not normally need to be done every year unless the soil is very acid. Do not apply lime to the area where potatoes are to be grown.

**Begin digging the vegetable plot** as crops are cleared. This is a job that needs to be tackled in small doses unless you are very fit.

**Make a note of particular crops** and varieties that did very well, and also those that are not worth bothering with again, while they are relatively fresh in your mind. The new season's seed catalogues will have arrived, and it is time to start planning for next year.

◀ Schizanthus, often known as poor man's orchid, makes a showy greenhouse plant with brightly coloured flowers and ferny foliage. It is not difficult to grow.

▲ Berries provide colour and interest throughout the autumn and much of the winter. *Pyracantha* 'Mojave' is an excellent and reliable variety.

65

## GREENHOUSE AND HOUSE PLANTS

**Sow sweet peas.** For the best plants and flowers next year, make a sowing of sweet peas now. Space the seeds well apart in pots of seed and cuttings compost, having first nicked the seed coat with a knife opposite the scar (this helps speed germination). Keep the seedlings in cool, well-ventilated, bright conditions.

There are many varieties of sweet pea available, some for exhibitors and specialists, some to provide cut flowers, and some for garden decoration. Most are sweetly scented.

| · SWEET PEA SELECTION · | |
|---|---|
| **Variety** | **Description** |
| 'Blaze' | Deep orange-scarlet, unfading blooms; lightly scented. |
| 'Candy' | Large, silver-grey flowers with delicate maroon markings; scented. |
| 'Cream Southbourne' | Very large, frilled cream flowers on long stems; vigorous grower, strongly scented. |
| 'Diamond Wedding' | White blooms on very long stems; ideal for cutting; strongly scented. |
| 'Fergus' | Large, deep carmine flowers with lighter keel; strong grower. |
| 'Midnight' | Very deep maroon, almost black, frilled flowers. |
| 'Mrs Bernard Jones' | Very large, pink and white flowers; strongly scented. |
| 'Old-Fashioned Mixed' | Small but very dainty, particularly fragrant flowers in a range of colours. |
| 'Queen Mother' | Lightly veined, soft salmon-orange, waved blooms; scented. |
| 'Red Arrow' | Large, deep scarlet, well-shaped flowers on strong stems. |

**Box up mint roots** to give a supply of young shoots in the winter. Fill seed trays with a loam-based potting compost or good garden soil, and dig up a number of the long, running roots of mint which can be found just below the surface. Cut these into suitable-sized sections and lay them on the surface of the seed tray, covering them very lightly with compost. Keep them just moist in a warm greenhouse or on a light windowsill in the home, where they will soon produce new shoots.

**Pot up annuals** being grown for spring flowers and set them in a light, cool position. Pinch out the tips of the shoots to encourage compact, bushy plants. Keep the compost just moist.

Many of these annuals are grown for their colourful flower display. The poor man's orchid (schizanthus) is very popular, with its light, ferny leaves and abundant flowers in shades of red, pink and rose; the bright, open, yellow and white flowers of poached egg plant (*Limnanthes douglasii*) are more commonly seen outside but also do well under cover. Mignonette, on the other hand, insignificant green flower spikes, but is worth growing for its beautiful violet scent.

**Greenhouse heating** will need to be started in most places now to keep greenhouses frost free, though this does depend on location. Thermostatically controlled systems present no problems as they can be switched on ready to cut in automatically when the temperature falls. Gardeners relying on less advanced heating systems will need to listen carefully to weather forecasts.

**Double glazing the greenhouse** with polythene is a good way to save a little on fuel bills in heated houses, and to give a little extra protection to plants in unheated houses. 'Bubble' polythene is the best material – preferably the type with large bubbles. It is bought in rolls, and should be put up horizontally, overlapping or taping the joints for maximum efficiency.

# Late Autumn

## FLOWERS AND ORNAMENTALS

**Plant trees and shrubs.** The dormant season – from late autumn through to early spring – is the traditional planting time for trees and shrubs, and still has much to commend it, although avoid times when the soil is waterlogged or frozen. While container-grown subjects theoretically can be planted all year round, care is often needed to get them to establish well when planted in the growing season. Dormant plants have plenty of time to recover from the upheaval of replanting, and for traditional, bare-root plants the dormant season is really the only time they can be planted successfully.

Before planting, prepare the site well before the plants arrive, removing weed roots and digging the soil deeply to ensure good drainage and a free root run.

Dig a planting hole that is wide enough to take all the roots without cramping, and deep enough for the tree to be planted to the original soil mark on the trunk. There are several planting mixes available: usually a mixture of peat or other organic matter and slow-release fertilizers. These can be forked into the bottom of the planting hole, and are particularly helpful on poor soils. Set the tree in the hole, and if a stake is necessary position it now, before the hole is refilled, without damaging any of the roots. Refill the hole with fine soil, jogging the tree up and down gently to start with, to sift soil through the roots and avoid air pockets. Tread the soil firm as you gradually refill until the site is level.

**Staking trees** is often necessary in exposed gardens, or if for any reason the roots are not firmly established in the soil by the time autumn winds arrive. Bad staking, however, can do more harm than good.

Use a stout stake, tall enough to come just below the head of the tree. If possible, put it in place before planting, to avoid root damage. But if it has to be put in later, position it about 45 cm (18 in) away from the stem, and take care not to damage the branches when hammering the stake in the soil until it is completely firm. Saw off the top off the stake if it is above the base of the branches at this point.

Fix the tree to the stake with a proper, adjustable tree tie that will not chafe the trunk (see below). For young trees, position the tree tie about half way up the stem to allow some movement in the wind, as this helps to build up and strengthen the trunk. Remember to inspect and adjust the tie as necessary as the tree grows.

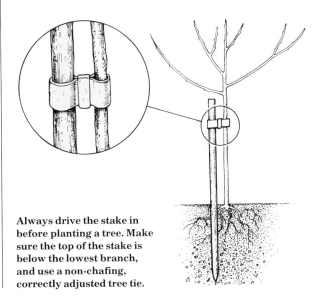

**Always drive the stake in before planting a tree. Make sure the top of the stake is below the lowest branch, and use a non-chafing, correctly adjusted tree tie.**

67

Continue tidying the herbaceous border, removing weeds, fallen leaves, dead flowers and so on. Spread well-rotted compost or manure on the soil between the plants if available; also around trees and shrubs, keeping it clear of the stems.

**Protect alpine plants** from rain. Plants with grey, woolly or furry leaves are affected by wet weather much more than by cold, and if rain collects in the crowns they will rot off and die. At the same time, there must be good movement of air around them, so they cannot be completely enclosed. Support a sheet of glass or clear acrylic over the tops of the plants, leaving the sides open. Sometimes woolly-leaved alpines are best grown in pots sunk in the soil, so that they can be lifted and overwintered in an unheated greenhouse or frame.

**Finish planting tulips and hyacinths.** These bulbs are better planted later than most of the other spring bulbs, but they should be planted as soon as possible now.

**Autumn-flowering plants** are always welcome to provide a little cheer at a time of year that can be depressing and dull. In any reasonably sheltered garden, schizostylis will now be producing its star-shaped flowers with their shining, satin-textured petals. The flowers are carried in groups on long stems which extend from iris-like leaves. 'Viscountess Byng' is a pink-flowered variety; 'Major' has large, deep red blooms. They make good cut flowers. Protect the crowns over winter with a layer of dry leaf litter or mound of straw.

◄ The bright, satin-textured petals of *Schizostylis coccinea* are a welcome sight in the autumn border. The plants' crowns may need a little protection to see them through the winter months.

► Autumn is the traditional planting time for trees and shrubs, though container-grown specimens can be planted all year round.

**Birds become hungry** as the first frosty days arrive, and berries on garden plants soon disappear. Large shrubs may be completely stripped after just a day or two of cold weather. Orange and yellow berries have the greatest chance of staying on the plants as they are less popular than red, but most gardeners who enjoy birdsong are philosophical about the plundering of the autumn display.

## FRUIT AND VEGETABLES

**Order seeds from catalogues.** The earlier you can get your order in, the more likely you are to receive all the varieties you want. Order a mixture of some new varieties and some old faithfuls you know perform well in your garden.

**Keep the vegetable plot tidy,** removing dead leaves, weeds etc. Debris provides shelter for overwintering pests.

# Winter pruning of fruit trees

Many gardeners are rather intimidated by the thought of fruit tree pruning, but it does not need to be complicated as long as you approach it methodically, and are clear about the reasons *why* you are pruning. These are:
- to remove dead, damaged and diseased wood
- to maintain a good framework of branches
- to promote fruiting shoots.

All cuts should be made just above, and sloping away from, a bud. Use well sharpened secateurs, and make clean cuts without snags.

**1.** The first step with any pruning job is to remove all dead, damaged and diseased wood, cutting it right back to healthy growth. Next, remove crossing branches that are rubbing against each other (or will be when they are weighed down with fruit). This will begin to clear the tree so that it becomes easier to see what to do next (see illustration).

**2.** Most free-standing fruit trees are grown as an open-centred cup shape, so that light and air can circulate freely around the branches and the fruits. If growth is crowded, thin it out, cutting branches back to a bud facing the direction in which you wish the shoot to grow. Try to keep the centre of the tree clear.

**3.** Cut laterals (side shoots) back if necessary to encourage the formation of fruiting spurs. Most will need reducing by about one-third of their length, but some can be cut back harder to an existing spur formation.

Remember that the harder you prune, the more vigorous will be the leafy growth the following year. A tree which is making a forest of shoots which bear little fruit should not be pruned hard in winter, no matter how tempting this seems. Prune lightly only, and restrict growth if necessary by summer pruning (see page 47).

Trained forms of fruit, such as cordons and espaliers, should have damaged wood removed in winter, and the leaders can be tipped back once they have reached the top of their supports, but their main pruning is carried out in summer, to restrict their growth. Plums should not be pruned in winter at all because there is more chance of the trees becoming infected with silver leaf disease in the dormant season.

**Start winter digging** as the ground becomes vacant. Digging is hard work, even on light soil, and should be done little and often (see page 78).

**Protect cauliflowers from frost** by breaking one of the large, outer leaves over the top of the curds.

**Begin harvesting winter vegetables** such as parsnips and sprouts. A good frost is said to improve the flavour, so traditionally these crops are not harvested until they have been frosted.

**Plan the vegetable plot for next season.** Crop rotation helps to avoid the build up of pests and diseases and takes account of different fertilizer requirements to help you to get the most from your crops.

There are various plans for rotations, but the simplest is to split the crops into brassicas (cabbage family), roots (such as carrots and beetroot) and everything else. (One of the drawbacks of following a rotation is that you need to grow roughly equal amounts of these three groups every year.) The plot that is to grow brassicas should receive an application of general fertilizer and lime (unless the soil is chalky); the roots plot should receive general fertilizer only, and the third plot should receive well-rotted manure, dug into the soil in winter.

The plots should rotate as follows:

|        | Plot 1    | Plot 2    | Plot 3    |
|--------|-----------|-----------|-----------|
| Year 1 | Brassicas | Roots     | Others    |
| Year 2 | Roots     | Others    | Brassicas |
| Year 3 | Others    | Brassicas | Roots     |

**Sow broad beans and hardy peas.** These crops will usually overwinter well in a reasonably sheltered position and give a very early harvest the following year. The variety of broad bean generally recommended for this late sowing is 'Aquadulce Claudia'; suitable peas are 'Feltham First' and 'Meteor'. Most seed catalogues mention other varieties that can be tried, too.

**Rhubarb can be forced** for early, tender crops, either in a greenhouse or outside. For greenhouse forcing, lift a root and leave it on the soil surface for a day or two to be frosted. Place it in a box of compost or good garden soil, water and put it in a warm greenhouse. Exclude all light from the developing shoots to keep them tender.

**Prune fruit trees** except when the weather is very frosty.

**Plant fruit trees,** treating them as for ornamental trees.

## GREENHOUSE AND HOUSE PLANTS

**Plant 'Paperwhite' narcissi bulbs** in bowls for sweet-scented, pure white, star-shaped flowers six weeks later. These bulbs do not need to be kept in the dark, but can be stood in a cool, light place immediately after planting. A greenhouse provides the best conditions, bringing the bulbs indoors just as the buds are opening (see below).

'Paperwhite' narcissi bulbs are unusual in that they need no dark period after planting. They will flower within six or seven weeks (see picture on page 72).

71

**Check bulbs in plunge beds** and bring them into the greenhouse and home as they become ready.

**Check temperatures** in the greenhouse regularly to ensure that the heating is doing its job properly. A maximum/minimum thermometer is an essential aid.

**Reduce the amount of watering** as the weather becomes colder and plant growth slows down. Take care not to splash water on plants or you will increase the risk of fungus diseases occurring.

**Grow quick and easy salads** by sowing sprouting seeds in a jam jar. Place a tablespoon of the seeds in the jar, cover with water and leave to soak for an hour. Cover the mouth of the jar with fine mesh net secured with an elastic band, then drain off the water. Rinse and drain the seeds thoroughly every day; within a few days they will have grown enough to fill the jar, when they can be eaten. Keep them out of sunlight for the tenderest sprouts. Try a range of the many different types available from seed merchants.

▼ The pure white flowers of narcissus 'Paperwhite' have the bonus of a very strong sweet scent.

▶ The garden on a cold winter's day has its own special beauty. With good planning, winter need never be a dull season.

◀ Sprouting seeds such as alfalfa take just a few days to grow in a jam jar. They make the perfect salad vegetable for autumn and winter.

# · 4 ·
# Winter

It is all too easy to let winter become a depressing time. The days are short, with dusk coming early; the weather is dull and damp or icy cold; plants in the garden are lifeless and stark.

But with a little planning, there is much that can be done to make winter an altogether more cheerful time. A backbone of evergreens ensures there is always some foliage to soften outlines, and gold-splashed variegated shrubs bring sunshine to the dreariest day. Even bare twigs can be attractive. The corkscrew hazel (*Corylus avellena contorta*) and contorted willow (*Salix matsudana tortuosa*) have wonderfully twisted and spiralling branches that make bold, eccentric outlines against a clear winter sky. Other willows, and dogwoods, produce thickets of shining red and yellow stems.

The trunks of trees come into their own: the flaking bark of eucalyptus in broad pools of cream and grey, or *Prunus serrula*, whose stem has a deep, glowing lustre like the patina of antique wood. Even the common birch stands out, with its delicate tracery of weeping branches and white bark shining in winter sun.

There are many winter flowers, too, and an astonishing number of them are powerfully scented. Everyone is familiar with the summer perfume of the rambling honeysuckle, but not so many know its winter-flowering cousins, *Lonicera fragrantissima, L. standishii* or *L. × purpusii*. These are shrubs, not climbers, and while the white flowers are not particularly showy, they have a delicious citrus scent. The pale lilac heads of *Daphne odora* are displayed against evergreen foliage (cream-margined in the hardiest version) but the mezereon (*Daphne mezereum*) carries its deep pink flowers thickly clustered on the leafless stems. Both waft sweet scents in the cold air. Then there's the winter-flowering viburnums, whose scent can stop you in your tracks yards away, and witch hazels, that carry flowers like ragged yellow spiders.

Winter jasmine is not scented, but its starry yellow flowers are a cheerful sight spangled across a wall. Flowering cherries are something to look forward to in spring: remind yourself of what is to come with *Prunus subhirtella* 'Autumnalis', a cherry that produces delicate white flowers throughout the winter, though with more polite restraint than the profusion of spring blossom.

There are other winter delights, too; the long tassels of garrya catkins, silvery-grey against a background of dark leaves, and, if the birds haven't finished them off, the still-glowing berries of many varieties hanging on from autumn.

The shortest day arrives quite early, and from then on we know that although the worst of the weather may be to come, we are on our way towards spring. Winter is a time of planning, of taking stock, of preparation for the growing season ahead.

# Early Winter

## FLOWERS AND ORNAMENTALS

**Protect tender plants.** The type of plants that need winter protection depends very much on where you live and the particular climate in your garden. In warm areas you may have tried plants such as carpenteria, passion flower, myrtle and campsis; these will need protection if they are to survive winter frosts.

In all but very favoured areas, plants such as ceanothus, rosemary, romneya, fuchsias, camellias, cistus, abelia and others will need help to survive the winters, particularly when newly planted. Once well established, it is surprising how hardy some of these plants can be, but a prolonged cold spell can wreak havoc even among established plants.

First of all, plant anything dubiously hardy in the right place. Warmth, sun and shelter from cold winds are required; the base of a south-facing wall is often ideal, but shelter can be provided by other, evergreen plants. Do not plant too shallowly; a good depth of soil over the roots will protect them. Top growth may be completely killed in cold weather, but the roots will often survive.

At the beginning of winter, mulch the root area with a deep layer or mound of peat, dry leaves, straw or similar insulating material. Protect top growth with temporary windbreaks (sacking supported on sturdy canes, for example) or pack round really tender plants with loose straw held in place by a wire netting surround. Always let some air get to the plant.

## Choosing a greenhouse

A greenhouse makes a great deal of difference to your gardening, enabling you to grow a whole new range of plants. It is particularly useful if it can be heated sufficiently to keep it frost free.

The framework may be wooden or aluminium, or occasionally plastic. Aluminium frames are cheaper and need no maintenance but the appearance of wood is preferred by some. Red cedar is the best choice; it should be treated with a wood preservative regularly. Greenhouses may have glass to ground level, or have a solid base of wood or brickwork on one or both sides (see below). Slatted staging on one side will increase the versatility of the house.

Always buy the largest size greenhouse you can afford. Site it in full sun if possible, and a convenient distance from the house. If possible, run an electricity cable to the site before construction, as electric heating is by far the most convenient method.

Ensure the site is level before construction. If you want a solid floor, use paving slabs, which can be taken up later if you decide you want a soil border.

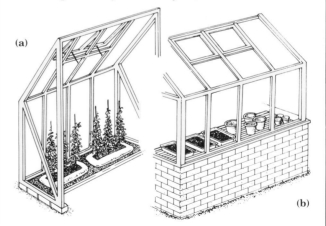

**Glass-to-ground greenhouses (a) are good for growing crops which require maximum light but are expensive to heat and may need shading in summer. A greenhouse with a solid base (b) can be fitted with staging for plants and seedlings, and the bricked area used for storage.**

If a precious plant appears to have been killed by frost, never be in too much of a hurry to dig it up. After very severe winters, roots have been known to remain dormant for up to a year before sending up new shoots.

**Continue tidying up borders.** Remember to leave dead stems and foliage where they might protect slightly tender plants, but not if the dead stuff is wet and rotting.

**Winter interest.** Now the leaves have all fallen, note whether the garden could be improved by the addition of more plants with interesting stems and branches.

**Prune off branches** that have been broken by autumn gales. Cut back cleanly to the main stem if necessary to preserve the shape of the plant, leaving a small collar of wood at the base of larger branches. Otherwise cut back to a bud which is facing in the direction in which you want new shoots to grow.

**Planting of bare-root and container-grown plants** can continue in all but frosty or very wet spells. There is often a very cold spell lasting up to a week or so in the early stages of the winter, but the weather usually then turns milder and wet.

If you are expecting bare-root shrubs or trees to arrive, keep a sheltered patch of well-dug soil (lightened with sand) covered over with plastic or similar material to protect it from rain and frost. This means you will have a workable patch in which to 'heel in' the plants temporarily if the ground is not suitable for setting them in their permanent positions. Alternatively, place the rootballs of the plants in a plastic sack and cover them with soil, peat or compost. On no account should the roots be allowed to dry out.

**Pruning of rose bushes** can begin now, but I prefer to leave it until late winter or very early spring. That way there is no die-back after

pruning to worry about, and it becomes more obvious which are live and healthy buds to cut back to.

**If garden ponds freeze over** for more than a day, thaw a hole in the ice to let gases escape. Do not break the ice with a hammer, as this could stun fish. Stand a metal saucepan filled with boiling water on the ice, or if it is very thick, use a blowlamp.

## FRUIT AND VEGETABLES

**Continue harvesting vegetable crops** such as kale, winter cabbages, parsnips, leeks, Brussels sprouts and so on. Remove dead foliage from plants as it is noticed.

**Lift some leeks and parsnips** and store in slightly moist soil in a box in a sheltered place near the kitchen. That way, if the soil is frozen hard so you cannot dig the vegetables out of the ground you will have some to hand.

**Check vegetables and fruit in store** regularly, using up those with blemishes first and removing any rotting ones.

**Continue digging the vegetable patch,** tackling it in small sections at a time if you are not used to digging. Add as much manure and compost as is available, but not in the areas in which you are going to grow root vegetables.

**Lift rhubarb roots for forcing.** If you want early, tender stems of rhubarb forced in the greenhouse, lift a root of rhubarb now and leave it on the soil surface, exposed to frosts.

**If you have cauliflowers** ready for harvest, protect the curds by breaking a leaf over the top of them.

**Jerusalem artichokes** are a useful winter vegetable. The knobbly tubers are something of an acquired taste, having a smoky flavour, but when well cooked are very pleasant. Start digging

**A greenhouse is a great asset for any keen gardener. Choose the largest size you can afford, and site it in full sun.**

the roots now, and try to remove every last tuber from the ground as you do so. Plants grow so strongly and rapidly from leftover roots that these 'volunteers' can become a real nuisance.

**Prune fruit trees.** Apples and pears can be pruned throughout the dormant season, but avoid frosty weather. First remove dying, dead and damaged wood – remember the three 'Ds' – and crossing branches. Then aim to keep the centre of the tree open, cutting out some shoots right back to their base. Shorten some of the side shoots to form fruiting spurs, but remember that winter pruning results in shoot growth. Pruning a tree too hard will mean a forest of new, unproductive shoots next spring. Summer pruning is the way to deal with excessive leafy growth.

77

# Winter digging

There are several reasons why we dig the soil:

- It enables us to remove residues of old crops, weeds and weed roots.
- It helps improve drainage.
- It facilitates the incorporation of organic matter.
- It exposes the maximum soil surface to winter frosts, which help break it down to fine crumbs.
- It exposes soil-living pests to predators such as birds.

On the minus side, digging can damage soil structure, and bring hosts of weed seeds near the surface where they can germinate. But on the whole, most gardeners carry out digging on a regular basis.

Heavy, clay soils need the most rigorous digging. The bottom of the trench can be broken up to improve drainage and the surface of the soil left in rough clods for winter frosts to break down. Light soils may not need such thorough digging, and can often simply be forked over in late winter or early spring, trying to invert each forkful of soil.

## Double digging

Double digging is very thorough, and good for heavy, badly drained or uncultivated soil, but it is hard work. A large plot needs tackling over an extended period unless you are very fit.

**1.** Dig the first trench to the depth of the spade (a spit) along the short axis of the plot. The soil from this trench should be put in a wheelbarrow and taken down to the furthest end of the plot (a).

**2.** Fork over the bottom of the trench, breaking up any hard 'pan' that may be present. Add organic matter such as well-rotted manure or garden compost (b).

**3.** Dig another trench one spit deep alongside the first, throwing the soil from this into the first trench to fill it up.

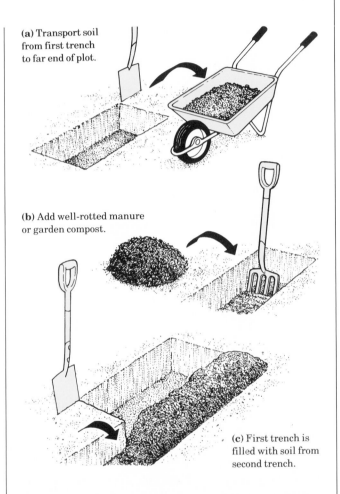

(a) Transport soil from first trench to far end of plot.

(b) Add well-rotted manure or garden compost.

(c) First trench is filled with soil from second trench.

**4.** Continue in this way down the whole length of the plot. Once you have dug the final trench, the soil barrowed down from the top of the plot can be used to fill it up (c).

## Single digging

This means digging a series of trenches one spit deep, but without forking over the soil at the base of the trench. The soil from each trench is thrown into the preceding one, as with double digging.

GREENHOUSE AND HOUSE PLANTS

**Continue planting bulbs of 'Paperwhite' narcissi** to flower through the winter. Plant batches every three or four weeks for a sucession of sweet-scented flowers.

**Before using the electricity supply** to the greenhouse, check that it is in good order, with no damaged cables. Fit an earth leakage circuit breaker to protect against electric shock. Check the greenhouse heaters are working properly with a maximum/minimum thermometer.

**Stop sweet peas sown in autumn,** pinching out the tips to keep the plants sturdy and bushy and prevent them becoming leggy. If you didn't sow seed in autumn, it can be sown now, in a propagator.

**There are plenty of winter-flowering pot plants** to cheer up the house and greenhouse at this time of year. Jasmine is a strong scrambling plant producing pure white flowers that can scent a whole room. Primroses in a wide range of colours are cheap and cheerful, and winter cherry bears a profusion of bright red or orange fruits. Christmas cactus and poinsettias are well known; apart from the usual bright red poinsettia, there are varieties with pink or white bracts, and one with variegated foliage. Cyclamen flowers come in a range of pink, red and white shades, and some varieties have quite a strong, peppery scent.

Light is at a premium these dull, short days, and many pot plants will appreciate a rest in a frost-free greenhouse after being in the house for a while. Plants which like cool conditions, such as cyclamen and Cape heaths, will be much happier there than in a centrally-heated home.

**Take care of newly-bought house plants** on the journey home from the shop. Being taken from the warmth of a store or garden centre into icy, windy streets can set them back severely.

# Buying garden tools

A basic garden tool kit consists of the following:
- *Spade* for digging. It may be full size or a 'border' spade, which is smaller and easier to use. Top-quality tools have stainless steel blades – long lasting and pleasant to use, but expensive.
- *Fork* for turning the soil over, and on very light soils may be used instead of a spade for digging. Again, a 'border' fork is smaller and lighter. A spade and fork may have wooden or plastic handles, and the top may be a T-shape, or more commonly a D-shape.
- *Rake* for breaking the soil surface down to fine crumbs, and bringing it level.
- *Hoe* – a Dutch hoe (a), with a well-sharpened blade, is for slicing weeds off at soil level. A draw hoe (b) is useful for drawing out drills when sowing seeds; it is only essential if you are a keen vegetable grower, but a good Dutch hoe is vital in all gardens.

**(a)** Dutch hoe  
**(b)** Draw hoe

- *Shears* for trimming hedges and lawn edges (long-handled are best for lawn edges).
- *Secateurs* for pruning (c and d).

**(d)** Parrot bill secateurs  
**(c)** Anvil secateurs

- *Trowel* for planting. Buy a good quality brand or you may find the handle bends as you apply leverage.

With all tools, always try them out and make sure they are comfortable to use before buying.

◀ The attractive flowers of *Iris unguicularis* appear throughout the winter. They have a strong, sweet perfume and are excellent for cutting.

▲ Bring forced bulbs from plunge beds into a greenhouse as soon as the first few centimetres of leaves are showing.

Most stores now supply large, shaped plastic bags which cover the whole plant and protect it from draughts, but the quicker the plant can be got home, the better.

**Foliage house plants** do a good job in providing interest the whole year round, and are especially appreciated now. Water them carefully, never giving them too much, but remember that plants in warm rooms may still be growing slowly. Clean the leaves, not forgetting the undersides. Remove yellowing foliage promptly – it is often a sign of overwatering in winter.

**Indoor plants** often do well on windowsills in winter, where the light is at its best, but don't draw the curtains in front of them on chilly nights. Shut off from the warmth of the room, they could be badly damaged by cold.

**Keep annuals** that have been sown in the greenhouse in good light. Water sparingly.

**Bring bulbs into the greenhouse** from plunge beds as soon as they are ready – showing about 5 cm (2 in) of leaf.

# Soil types

The soil is one of the most important aspects of growing any plants. If you have been getting unsatisfactory results from your garden, or have moved to a new garden, it is worth looking a little deeper into what makes up the soil there.

Soil is generally rock which has been weathered to fine particles over many thousands of years, plus the remains of plants and animals that have lived there. In the same way that different regions have different types of rock, they also have different types of soil. Soil types can vary within quite a small area – even within the same garden.

The best way to start finding out about your soil is to dig a 'profile pit' – a straight-sided hole up to 1.5 m (4 ft) deep if you can manage it. From this you should be able to see distinct bands of different types of soil, and how deep each band is. You now know

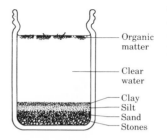

Thoroughly shake a trowelful of garden soil up with water in a jam jar and leave it for several days to settle. The sediments settle out in different layers, enabling you to see the varying proportions of your soil – whether it is mainly clay or sand, for example.

- Organic matter
- Clear water
- Clay
- Silt
- Sand
- Stones

whether the soil is shallow and over chalk, or has clay beneath which may impede drainage, and so on.

The soil in the top 30 cm (1 ft) or so is the most important, for it is here that the majority of roots exist. Dig up a handful of soil and moisten it if necessary, then squeeze it. Try to roll it into a ball, then into a long sausage shape. Try to join the two ends of the sausage to make a ring.

Break off a small piece of soil and add enough water to make it fairly wet. Rub the soil between thumb and forefinger. Does it feel gritty, or sticky, or slippery?

The main types of soil are clay, sand and silt, though most soils are a mixture of the three (loam), in varying proportions.

**Clay**    Will form a lump when squeezed and can be rolled into a ball. The surface of the ball may be polished with a finger. It will roll into a sausage shape which can be joined to form a ring. Feels sticky when rubbed between the fingers.

**Sandy**    Will not form a ball, but falls apart when squeezed. Feels gritty.

**Silt**    Feels silky or slippery when rubbed between the fingers. May form a ball if it also contains clay.

From this you can classify your soil as a type of 'loam' such as sandy loam (predominantly sandy), clay loam (predominantly clay), or even sandy clay loam (a mixture of clay and sand).

The degree of soil acidity or alkalinity, known as the pH, should be ascertained by carrying out a simple soil test.

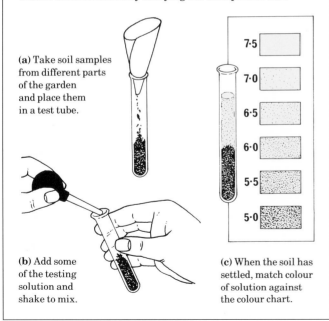

**(a)** Take soil samples from different parts of the garden and place them in a test tube.

**(b)** Add some of the testing solution and shake to mix.

**(c)** When the soil has settled, match colour of solution against the colour chart.

7·5
7·0
6·5
6·0
5·5
5·0

# Mid-Winter

## FLOWERS AND ORNAMENTALS

**Take root cuttings of poppies.** Poppy plants are quite easy to propagate by this method. The plants can be dug up entirely if you wish to make a large number of cuttings, but you can make a reasonable amount without disturbing the parent plant. Carefully scrape the soil away at one side of the plant until you expose the roots, and cut off one or two roots of about pencil thickness. Cut these into sections around 5 cm (2 in) long, being careful to keep them the right way up; it is normal to make a sloping cut at the base of the cutting and a straight cut across the top. Insert the cuttings into a pot or deep tray of moist, gritty compost topped off with a layer of sand, until the tops are level with the surface. Place them preferably in a cold frame, and keep the soil just moist until shoots begin to grow in spring.

Other plants that can be propagated from root cuttings include phlox, gaillardia, anchusa, verbascum and romneya. In some cases their roots are too thin to be inserted upright, and should be laid flat on the surface of the compost and just lightly covered.

**Planting can continue** throughout the winter whenever the soil conditions and weather allow.

**Weeds continue to grow** in mild spells throughout the winter, and should be removed occasionally as they are seen. Prick over the soil between plants in borders as you remove the weeds.

**Foliage of some spring-flowering bulbs** will soon be appearing: that of grape hyacinths (muscari) is usually well advanced already. Be careful not to damage young shoots emerging through the soil. *Iris unguicularis* makes an untidy jumble of foliage for most of the year, but now it is producing its lovely, short-stemmed blue flowers that earn it its place in any garden. Flowers will carry on being produced throughout the winter, despite the weather. They are good for cutting, though some people find their strong, sweet scent almost overwhelming. A well-drained, thin soil produces the most flowers.

**Lily bulbs** are often not available until midwinter, but there is still time to plant them

| · TREES VALUABLE FOR THEIR WINTER BARK · | |
|---|---|
| **Name** | **Description** |
| *Acer capillipes* | A 'snake bark' maple, with brown bark streaked white; young growths red. |
| *Acer griseum* | Paperbark maple; bark peels and curls attractively to reveal shining, cinnamon-brown new wood beneath. |
| *Arbutus × andrachnoides* | An unusual strawberry tree with strikingly marked, peeling, warm brown bark. |
| *Betula jacquemontii* | A lovely birch with dazzling white bark. |
| *Betula nigra* | River birch; bark is at first pink-tinged white but turns darker and shaggy. |
| *Betula papyrifera* | The paperbark birch has white bark peeling in shaggy, papery layers. |
| *Betula pendula* | The common silver birch should not be forgotten; its shining white stems marked with black are always attractive. |
| *Eucalyptus dalrympleana* | A hardy plant with attractive patchworked, light-coloured bark. |
| *Eucalyptus gunnii* | One of the most popular and hardy eucalypts; fast growing, with well-marked, smooth bark in varying shades of buff, cream and grey. |
| *Eucalyptus niphophila* | Bark like a snake's skin in grey, cream and green patches. |
| *Prunus serrula* | Brilliantly glossy, warm reddish-brown trunk. |

outside. The big bulbs should be bought as soon as you see them, and not kept out of the soil any longer than necessary, or they will shrivel. If the weather is not suitable for planting, pot them up in just-moist compost.

**Continue to thaw a hole in the ice** on garden ponds if the water remains frozen for more than a day. This lets toxic gases escape from the water.

**Order flower seeds** from the seed catalogues. Don't get carried away – make sure you know where all the plants are to grow before you spend a fortune ordering seeds you really have no room for in the garden.

**After frosts,** check recently planted trees and shrubs to ensure they have not had their roots lifted by the frost. Firm them in by gently treading round them.

**If heavy snow falls,** shake or knock it off the branches of evergreen trees before the weight breaks them.

## LAWNS

**Keep off the lawn in frosty weather.** Walking on frozen grass kills it, and blackened footprints will soon be the evidence.

**Natural pathways across grass** may not show up in other seasons, but the grass soon becomes thin where it is constantly walked on in wet, cold weather. Spike compacted turf areas with a fork, and try to persuade people to take another route. If this is a continual problem, consider laying stepping stones or another type of path to replace the lawn in that area.

**Brush away dead leaves** and other debris that collects in corners of the lawn, before it smothers the grass.

◀ The brilliant, shining red bark of *Prunus serrula* catches the winter sun to give a warm glow to the winter garden.

Stepping stones or a similar firm path will prevent grass being worn away by constant treading in winter. Make sure the path follows a convenient route or it may not be used.

**Send lawnmowers, hedge-trimmers and other garden machinery away for sharpening and servicing.** As soon as the lawn needs its first trim in spring, garden tool repairers are flooded out with forgotten machines, meaning long delays for customers.

**Clean garden tools and sharpen them.** Check that spades, forks etc. have had all the soil cleaned off them, and give metal surfaces a rub over with an oily rag. Spades and hoes should be sharpened with a file to give them a good edge. Rub down wooden handles in case there are splinters.

# Laying paving

A paved area provides a firm, all-weather surface in the garden, and is a suitable base for garden furniture, or for areas that receive too much traffic for turf. Uneven paving is a potential hazard and a permanent irritation, so it is worth taking trouble to do the job properly.

There is a wide range of paving materials available, but slabs are probably the most popular. These may be plain, pre-cast concrete in a variety of colours, or 'riven' concrete that gives a very realistic impression of natural stone. Concrete slabs may also be impressed with various designs to give an appearance of cobbles or bricks, for instance. Then there are reconstituted stone slabs, and, most expensively, natural stone. These are all available in a variety of sizes and shapes.

Excavate and level the area to be paved, allowing for a depth of 10 cm (4 in) of hardcore plus 5 cm (2 in) sharp sand, plus the thickness of the slabs – generally either 5 cm (2 in) or 6.5 cm (2½ in). Make levelling pegs from wooden stakes, marking the pegs with the levels of hardcore and sand, so that the top of the pegs will be level with the base of the paving slabs. Hammer the pegs in about 2 m (6 ft) apart over the area to be paved, using a spirit level to keep the tops level. Allow a fall of 1:60 for drainage away from the house.

Fill the excavated area with hardcore to the lower level on the pegs, then with sharp sand to their tops (a). Mark the exact edges of the paved area with taut string, and begin laying the slabs alongside the house wall. Bed each slab on five mortar spots and drop the slab into position – do not try to push it into place. Check the levels regularly with a spirit level and adjust the slabs if necessary by tapping them gently with the base of a club hammer (b). Slabs may be butted up or a 1 cm (½ in) space left between them for pointing. Lay the second row of slabs at right angles to the first, then continue filling the area in. Avoid walking on newly laid slabs. After a day or two, brush in a dry mortar mix, working it well into the cracks. Make sure the surface of the slabs is dry before you do this, and brush off all traces of the mortar mix from them afterwards.

**(a)**

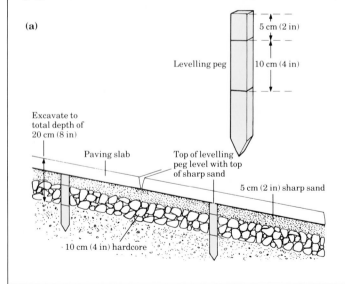

5 cm (2 in)

Levelling peg

10 cm (4 in)

Excavate to total depth of 20 cm (8 in)

Paving slab

Top of levelling peg level with top of sharp sand

5 cm (2 in) sharp sand

10 cm (4 in) hardcore

**(b)**

Position of 5 spots of mortar for next slab

## FRUIT AND VEGETABLES

**Continue digging** over the vegetable garden.

**Order vegetable seeds and seed potatoes.** As with flower seeds, make sure you order only what you have room for. Practise crop rotation to avoid disease build-up.

**Continue to force rhubarb.** This can be done simply by covering the crown with an old dustbin or box: pack it lightly with straw for extra insulation and early sticks. An old-fashioned forcing pot can also be used, and is an attractive way to do the job. Alternatively, frosted roots can be brought into the greenhouse, boxed up in compost and covered so that light does not get at the sticks (see illustration). The extra warmth will mean very early crops.

**Continue to harvest vegetables** that are available. Many people believe that leeks, Brussels sprouts, swedes and parsnips should not be eaten until they have been well frosted, as this is thought to improve the flavour.

**Mulch asparagus beds** with a thick layer of well-rotted compost or manure. Remove any perennial weeds that may be present first.

**Continue pruning fruit trees,** aiming to get the job finished as soon as possible now.

**Inspect fruit and vegetables** in store regularly.

**Rabbits can do a great deal of damage** by stripping the bark off young trees during cold spells. They are mainly a problem in rural and semi-rural areas. Once the bark has been removed all the way round the stem, the tree will die. Ensure trees are protected with rabbit guards or wire netting.

**Protect fruit buds** from attack by birds. Bullfinches are responsible for much of the damage, though other small birds do their share. Various proprietary bird-scaring and deterring products are available.

Forcing rhubarb by excluding all light produces an early crop of very tender sticks.

(a) Dig up the crown and cut into three or four sections, each with a growing point.

(b) Place the crowns in boxes of compost of good garden soil and put them under the greenhouse staging.

(c) Surround the box with sacking or black material to exclude light from the developing stems.

A forcing pot lightly filled with straw can be placed over rhubarb crowns outside: the lid can be removed to check how sticks are developing. They will not be as early as those forced in a warm greenhouse.

▲ Many gardeners delay harvesting winter vegetables such as Brussels sprouts because they believe a good frosting will improve their flavour.

► Even in the depths of winter, a well-planned garden can provide striking colour and form.

## GREENHOUSE AND HOUSE PLANTS

**Wash seedtrays and pots** ready for the sowing season. Add a few drops of disinfectant to the water.

**Remove all dead leaves,** dead plants and other debris from the greenhouse. Clean the glass if necessary, to ensure maximum light transmission.

Unheated greenhouses which are empty or nearly so can be given a good spring clean, scrubbing down the framework, glass and staging. Choose a mild day when any plants which are in the greenhouse can be put outside while the work is being carried out.

**Continue bringing bulbs into the greenhouse** as they become ready.

**Use a maximum/minimum thermometer** to check that the heating system is working effectively.

**Keep the atmosphere as dry as possible,** ventilating on sunny days – an automatic ventilator is useful. Damp, cold, stagnant air encourages fungus diseases.

**Start chrysanthemum stools** into growth for taking cuttings. The stools, which should have been boxed up in dry compost, can now be watered and the heat increased if necessary. New shoots will soon arise to be used as cuttings.

**Prune back overwintering pelargoniums and fuchsias** and water them to start them into growth for taking cuttings. If the greenhouse is only just frost free, this can be delayed until late winter.

**If you have a heated propagator,** a number of seeds can be sown now – pelargoniums, *Begonia semperflorens*, and tomatoes among them. You should, however, delay the sowings a little if you do not think you can provide warm enough conditions for the developing seedlings later on.

**Fruit cages** should have the top mesh replaced with winter netting. This has a larger mesh so that snow can fall through it; the smaller mesh netting holds the snow, the weight of which can break it or even buckle the fruit cage supports. Unfortunately, the larger mesh netting does not keep out bud-pecking small birds.

## FLOWERS AND ORNAMENTALS

**Prune roses.** This is the best time to prune roses – while they are still dormant but shortly to break into growth. As always, remove the three D's first – dead, damaged and diseased wood. This applies to all the groups of roses below.

Hybrid tea varieties should be pruned hard, cutting stems back to a healthy, outward-facing bud within 5–10 cm (2–4 in), or two to four buds, of the main stem. Floribundas should be pruned rather more lightly, and species and old garden roses hardly at all, just enough to remove old wood and keep the plants shapely.

Climbing roses, which mainly flower on the current year's growth, should have a main framework of branches which can be lightly tipped back to keep it within bounds. Side shoots that spring from this main framework are pruned back to two buds, with weak shoots removed. Strong, vigorous growth can be left if required to extend or replace part of the main framework.

Rambling roses flower on older wood. Retain as many of the previous season's shoots as possible and cut out most of those that have flowered. If more shoots are required to cover the area on which the rose is growing, retain strong, healthy shoots that flowered last year, and cut back side shoots on these to two or three buds.

**Continue planting bare-root trees and shrubs,** but this should be finished as soon as possible now.

**A final tidy of the border** can take place when the worst of the winter weather is over. Remove dead top growth that has been left on to protect plants. This will also remove hiding places for slugs and snails which will be lying in wait for the juicy young shoots of the plants to show themselves in spring. Particularly vulnerable plants such as delphiniums and hostas can be protected by surrounding them with ashes or sharp grit, or alternatively by placing slug pellets under a tile nearby.

| · SHRUBS FOR WINTER SCENT · | |
|---|---|
| **Name** | **Description** |
| *Chimonanthus praecox* (wintersweet) | Waxy yellow flowers with a purple blotched centre are carried through the winter on established plants |
| *Choisya ternata* (Mexican orange blossom) | Clusters of starry, white, sweet-scented flowers at intervals throughout the winter, with the main flush in spring; the glossy evergreen foliage is also aromatic |
| *Daphne mezereum* (mezereon) | Dense clusters of strongly perfumed, purple flowers on upright, leafless branches in late winter; they are followed by poisonous red berries |
| *Daphne odora* | Small heads of fragrant purple blooms on an evergreen shrub; 'Aureomarginata' is the hardiest form |
| *Hamamelis mollis* (witch hazel) | Ragged yellow flowers on leafless branches in early and mid-winter; good autumn colour from the foliage, too |
| *Lonicera fragrantissima* (shrubby honeysuckle) | Pale cream, very fragrant flowers on a twiggy, semi-evergreen shrub; *L. purpusii* and *L. standishii* are similar |
| *Mahonia japonica* | Gently dangling racemes of sweetly fragrant, pale yellow flowers at the tips of evergreen stems all through the winter |

# Sowing indoors

Seeds are sown under protection for several reasons. They may be too tender to be sown outside safely until late in the spring; they may benefit from an early start to give them a longer growing season; they may need special care and attention which cannot be given outside, or they may be plants which are to spend their whole lives in a house or greenhouse. Sowing may take place in a greenhouse, propagator, or even on a bright windowsill in the home.

**1.** Fill a seedtray with seed compost, heaping it up and spreading it out to the corners well. Strike the compost off level with the edge of a presser (a piece of wood cut to fit the seed tray, with a handle attached). Then use the presser to firm the compost lightly in the tray (a).

**2.** Water the compost before sowing if it is dry, using a fine rose on the can (b) or standing the tray in water for several hours until the surface is moist.

**3.** Sow the seed thinly (c) over the surface of the compost, sprinkling it or tapping it out of the packet.

**4.** Cover the seed lightly with a further layer of sieved compost, vermiculite or silver sand. Some very fine seed should be left uncovered – check the instructions on the seed packet. Fine seed is easier to handle if it is mixed with a little silver sand before sowing, to act as a spreader.

**5.** If the compost is not already watered, water carefully now, using a very fine rose on the can to avoid disturbing the seed.

**6.** Cover the seedtray with a sheet of glass and a layer of newspaper (d), or (more simply) another seedtray inverted over the top (e).

**7.** Keep the tray in an even temperature, checking regularly to see whether the seeds have germinated and to make sure the compost remains just moist.

Once the majority of seeds have germinated, remove the newspaper or upturned seedtray. Remove the glass when the first seedling touches it.

**8.** Keep the seedlings in a bright position but shaded from direct sunlight, and keep the compost just moist at all times.

**9.** As soon as they are large enough to handle, prick the seedlings out into individual pots or space them further apart in another tray. Always handle them by their seed leaves, never by their stems.

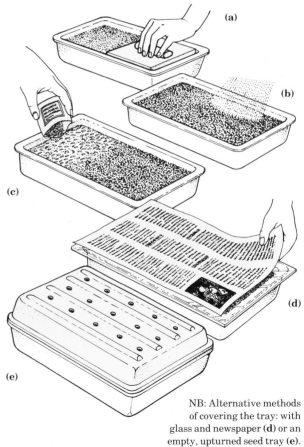

(a)

(b)

(c)

(d)

(e)

NB: Alternative methods of covering the tray: with glass and newspaper (**d**) or an empty, upturned seed tray (**e**).

◄ The ragged yellow blooms of witch hazel (*Hamamelis mollis*) are very sweetly scented. Plants provide good autumn leaf colour as a bonus.

► One of the most popular winter-flowering pot plants, poinsettias are available in pink and white forms as well as the better known red varieties.

## LAWNS

**Lawn edges** which have crumbled over winter can be repaired in mild weather now. Cut round the damaged section with a sharp edging iron to form a rectangle. Carefully lift the rectangle of turf and turn it 180°, so that the damaged section is on the opposite side to the lawn edge. Line the straight edge up carefully with the lawn edge and pat the turf into place. Fill in the damaged area with sifted soil and lawn seed.

**Send away lawnmovers for servicing** if you have not already done so.

**Lawn repairs.** If you can obtain a small number of turves, use them to replace any worn sections of the lawn that have fared badly over the winter and are unlikely to recover.

## FRUIT AND VEGETABLES

**Finish off digging the vegetable plot** as soon as possible.

**Sow early peas and broad beans** in sheltered positions, preferably under cloches.

**Lift remaining leeks, parsnips and swedes** before they start into growth again.

**Leafy Brussels sprouts tops** make a useful vegetable when all the sprouts have been picked. Uproot the stalks and burn them – they take too long to rot down on the compost heap.

**Plant out spring cabbages** when the weather is suitable. Lime the area for brassicas if necessary, as lime helps prevent clubroot disease.

**When seed potatoes arrive,** immediately set them rose-end (the end with the most eyes)

upward in seedtrays or egg cartons in a light, frost-free place. Strong, compact shoots will soon form, and these are less likely to be knocked off at planting time than the pale spindly shoots that arise in a dark place. Reduce the shoots to the two strongest as soon as possible.

**Plant shallots.** Although shallots are traditionally 'planted on the shortest day, harvested on the longest', this is a better time to plant them. Make a hole for the bulbs with a dibber or trowel. Just pushing them into the soil compacts the soil immediately below them, making it difficult for the roots to penetrate. The bulbs will then tend to push themselves out of the ground again when the roots begin to grow.

**It is often recommended to sow parsnips** very early in the year, but I have always had much more reliable crops from sowings in early or mid-spring. Parsnips take ages to germinate at the best of times: sow between each seed station with radishes as a marker crop.

**Autumn-fruiting raspberries** carry a crop on the current season's growth, unlike summer varieties which fruit on the previous year's canes. Prune the canes down to within 5 cm (2 in) of the ground now. If this is not done, however, the plants will just crop at the normal time instead of late summer and autumn.

Some varieties carry a rather variable autumn crop. If you have been disappointed in the past, it might be worth converting the plants to summer fruiting, when they could crop more heavily.

## GREENHOUSE AND HOUSE PLANTS

**Pot up autumn-sown annuals** as necessary.

**Start chrysanthemums, dahlias, pelargoniums and fuchsias** into growth if this has not already been done. Take cuttings from plants already producing shoots.

**Prune back** plants which have been overwintering, such as lemon verbena, bougainvillea, specimen fuchsias and pelargoniums. Cut to a healthy bud.

**Increase watering** as early plants start into growth, but be careful not to overwater.

**Look out for the first invasions of aphids** on soft young shoot tips. They are easily controlled by a short-persistence 'safe' insecticide such as pyrethrum or soft soap.

**Sow tomatoes, cucumbers and melons** for cropping in the greenhouse.

**Sow dwarf French beans and broad beans** in fibre pots for planting out later. Peas, cauliflowers and early cabbage can also be sown. Runner beans should be sown later, as they cannot be planted out until all risk of frost is over. Sown too early, they will become unwieldy and over-large.

**Sow quick-maturing carrots** to mature in the greenhouse border.

**Prick off seedlings** and pot up young plants as they become large enough.

**Begin sowing half-hardy annuals** for bedding. Ensure you have sufficient supplies of compost, labels, seedtrays and pots for the season ahead, and that trays and pots are clean.

**Start begonia tubers into growth.** Place the tubers dished side upwards in pots of moist compost; do not cover them, but leave the top surface, where hairy buds will soon be visible, above soil level. Give the tops a light misting of water just once to start them off: after that they must be kept dry to avoid rotting.

**Remove faded flowers from cyclamen** by grasping the flower stalks between finger and thumb and rolling them while pulling gently.

When all the foliage has died down the plants should be left in their pots and turned on their side for the tubers to dry out. They can be restarted into growth in mid- to late summer.

# Index

Page numbers in *italics* indicate an illustration, boxed table, special project or special technique.